Outdoor Careers

Exploring Occupations in Outdoor Fields

Ellen Shenk

Foreword by Robert Calvert, Jr.

STACKPOLE
BOOKS

Published by
STACKPOLE BOOKS
Cameron and Kelker Streets
P.O. Box 1831
Harrisburg, PA 17105

Cover design by Caroline Miller

Printed in the United States of America

First Edition

10 9 8 7 6 5 4 3

Library of Congress Cataloging-in-Publication Data

Shenk, Ellen.
    Outdoor careers : exploring occupations in outdoor fields / Ellen Shenk.
  — 1st ed.
      p.   cm.
    Includes bibliographical references and index.
    ISBN 0-8117-2542-1
    1. Vocational guidance.   2. Occupations.   3. Outdoor life—Vocational
guidance.   4. Outdoor recreation—Vocational guidance.
    I. Title
    HF5381.S542   1992
331.7'02—dc20   92-17530
                                            CIP

Contents

Foreword

Mark Twain once said that "the luckiest people in the world are those who get to do all year round what they most like to do during their summer vacation." No one can argue with that concept, and studies have shown that when they think of the ideal job, millions of Americans today would like one that is performed outdoors.

Outdoor jobs just don't grow on trees. The good ones are hard to find, and there is intense competition for those jobs that feature outdoor work and also offer a reasonable opportunity to develop into a substantial career. The need for accurate and up-to-date information on a variety of good jobs that can be performed outdoors prompted the development of this book.

Outdoor jobs, as this realistic text points out, are not likely to provide you with the wherewithal to finance a condo in Laguna Beach, a Mercedes in the driveway, or maybe even sufficient resources to send your children to Ivy League colleges. But outdoor jobs feature a lot of satisfaction, are likely to keep you in much better physical condition than many of your contemporaries, can provide sufficient income for life's necessities, and generally provide the feeling that what you do contributes to a cause in which you believe strongly.

Many of the outdoor jobs profiled in this book help to protect and sustain our environment and thus play a significant role in the attempt to save our planet for future generations. People have discovered that what happens to the tropical rain forests may affect the quality of air in Boston, that steel mills in our Midwest contribute to the acid rain that impacts on fishing in Quebec, and that the sediment from fertilizers and pesticides used on French and Italian farms runs down rivers and is affecting the quality of life in the Mediterranean.

A recent international conference noted that the current threat to our environment may be as extreme as the conditions that killed off the dinosaurs many millenia ago. And unless radical changes are made, from 10 to 20 percent of the estimated ten million species of plants and animals will be extinct by the year 2020. Many of the outdoor careers cited in this book help to preserve and protect our environment. Others sustain interest in environmental concerns by focusing attention on the world in which we live.

The area of outdoor careers is fortunate to have an author of the stature of Ellen Shenk to research its opportunities and to identify the significant number of fields that offer real career opportunities. Whether you are reading about the young woman who works as an elephant trainer, the young man who works as a ski patroller, or the woman who makes her career in aquaculture, you sense that real people are finding interesting and exciting careers in outdoor fields.

Thanks to this book, the biggest problem for many readers may not be the decision to pursue an outdoor career, but which of the many fascinating options to consider.

Robert Calvert, Jr.
Editor
Career Opportunities News

Acknowledgments

I thank many people for their assistance in the process of completing this book. Persons in various careers shared information and gave their perspectives on their daily work; many others from organizations across the country sent helpful materials. My business partner, Violet Houser, gave editing and organizational assistance. Gloria Monick's comments on the career and job search chapters were invaluable. Above all, I give special thanks to my family and friends. Their support, understanding, and encouragement were important ingredients in the completion of this long project.

*"There is a presence and an influence in Nature and the Open
which expands the mind and causes brigand cares and worries to
drop off—whereas in confined places foolish and futile thoughts
of all kinds swarm like microbes and cloud and conceal the soul."*

Edward Carpenter

Introduction

The lure of the outdoors and of work in the outdoors is a great attraction for many people. This book is addressed to those of you who want to explore how an interest in the outdoors may affect your career choice. All of the careers covered relate in some way to the outdoors, either involving a significant amount of work outside or building on outdoor interests.

Two of the words used in this book must be clarified. The term *outdoors* is used as defined by Webster: "out of doors; in the open air." The use of the word *career* follows another Webster definition: "profession." *Career, occupation,* and *job* are used interchangeably today and throughout this book. Because *career* is now receiving the widest usage, it has been selected for the book title.

This book will introduce the major areas of outdoor work and provide information about a number of careers available in each one. It is intended to make you aware of the many options and opportunities and to help give you direction in choosing a career.

How to Use This Book

A book of this size cannot pretend to be the last word on the subject. It is intended to be a starting point, not the final destination. But it should expand your horizons, help focus your career search, and give you ideas of places to go for more information.

1

Related careers are grouped in chapters under general headings. The careers are also listed in the index by title. If you are looking for a specific occupation and want to find it quickly, check the index. Reading the whole book, however, may open up additional options you hadn't previously considered, so don't be too hasty in zeroing in on specific information.

Persons in various professions have been profiled to put a human face on the career descriptions and give a glimpse of how different people feel about their work. Reading about how these persons have found their way and what they do, along with their advice, should give you ideas and information to aid your search for a career that fits your special interests and abilities.

The book also includes critical information about the process of choosing a career and conducting a job search, as well as listings of resources where more knowledge about these careers can be obtained. Selecting a career and the job search have been the focus of entire books, however, and you may wish to research further using the suggested books.

One caution: Be aware of the limitations of the printed page. Every effort has been made to obtain up-to-date information for this book, but careers respond very quickly to changing economic conditions. In a volatile economic climate, career information is subject to change, particularly regarding salaries and the numbers of positions available.

Additionally, salaries vary widely depending on the size and type of employer and on local economic forces. Although all attempts have been made to obtain accurate salary figures, there will be variations between localities. The figures given should provide you with an idea of what the salary range may be. Use this book as a guide, not the last word.

Seasonal Outdoor Work

Many people are able to find satisfactory full-time employment in outdoor careers by creatively combining several career options. The conservation and recreation fields offer many part-time or seasonal jobs. The chapters on these areas give some information about seasonal work and list specific resources. Part-time possibilities do exist in other fields, however, so anyone looking for an outdoor career should consider the possibility of utilizing part-time work in the search for a perfect job fit.

Bob Birkby, who is profiled in chapter 9, has found writing to be complementary to rigorous summer outdoor positions. From his own experience Birkby offers some advice for persons looking for outdoor work: "People interested in full-time outdoor careers have a tough challenge ahead. The agencies [such as the Student Conservation Association] don't have many openings these days, and their hiring guidelines cause opportunities to be even more limited.

"Seasonal outdoor work is much more accessible, and it allows people to build up experience that can make them more qualified for full-time employment. Some mountaineers I've worked with went through NOLS [National Outdoor Leadership School] training, and then became NOLS instructors before forming their own company. The Student Conservation Association hires fifty to sixty supervisors each summer for its high school programs, and it places close to a thousand volunteers in twelve-week resource assistant internships with agencies all over America.

"Having a special skill can make a person much more marketable. In my case, my trail construction expertise has opened lots of doors. During the summers I spent at Philmont [a Boy Scout camp in New Mexico] learning trail work, I earned barely enough to cover my expenses, but I think that's going to be the case when learning most outdoor skills. Lots of people want to do this sort of thing, and many are willing to do anything for a while to make it happen. That means the entry-level and apprenticeship positions don't pay much, and until a person has some significant experience under his or her belt, moving beyond those temporary, low-paying jobs is not very easy."

Several organizations offer training or some positions in outdoor or wilderness skills. The National Outdoor Leadership School teaches wilderness skills and leadership with emphasis on conservation and ethics. It also holds educational conferences and seminars and does publishing and research on wilderness-related topics. Outward Bound is an educational program that uses challenging wilderness activities to train for leadership and assist with self-discovery. It operates several schools throughout the country and has about one thousand seasonal employees and fewer than two hundred full-time employees.

The Appalachian Mountain Club offers a variety of employment opportunities in trail work, education, facilities and hotel management, and other related fields. The Student Conservation Association gives opportunities for high school and adult volunteers to work on conservation projects across the country. This provides some jobs for both leading the volunteers and exposing them to a variety of conservation careers. Addresses for these four organizations are listed in the Resources section at the end of this chapter.

Additional Outdoor Fields

The scope of this book does not allow for coverage of all occupations that involve work in the outdoors. Some, such as military careers, were deliberately omitted. Although all branches of the military offer varied jobs in the outdoors, they are not included in this book because the ultimate choice of job assignment belongs with the military, not with the individual.

Law enforcement is another career that, depending upon the type of job and the location, offers a fair amount of work outdoors in all types of weather. Increasingly, law enforcement positions are available in the National Parks, as mentioned in chapter 4. Many people find that this work offers rewards from helping others and satisfaction because the work is so important. Reasons for choosing careers in law enforcement seldom include working in the outdoors, however.

Anthropology is another field that usually involves some work in the outdoors. A social science, anthropology examines the origins, the physical development, and cultures of human beings. Although anthropologists work in universities, colleges, and museums, most also do field work in places as diverse as the Arctic and Africa. Linguistic anthropologists, who study the development of languages, may spend time visiting tribes that have no written languages. Cultural anthropologists often study groups or tribes of people; they conduct their research by interviewing people and observing their behavior.

Archaeology, a subfield of anthropology, studies human societies by examining articles such as tools, art, artifacts, and utensils. Archaeologists go to locations that housed early cities, cemeteries, or dumping grounds to study. They often spend long hours sifting painstakingly through sand or soil, sometimes in remote locations with crude living conditions.

Second Careers

Many people wishing to change jobs seriously consider outdoor work as part of a second (or even third) career. They have discovered while working at other careers that outdoor-type work is important for them. If this describes you, use the information you have learned about yourself on previous jobs as you read through this book to find an appropriate career in the outdoors.

Unfortunately, many outdoor jobs do not pay well; often, one of the major rewards of the career is simply being able to work in the outdoors. Persons who have retired early from government or military service and have a full pension may be better able to take the lower salary than others who do not have the benefit of a secondary income.

Where to Go from Here

You may wish to obtain some of the materials listed in the Resources section at the end of each chapter. Another excellent way to get career information is to contact persons who are currently working in the field that interests you. A personal interview would be preferable, but depending on where you live, you may find it better to write. Because work settings play an important part in someone's reaction to a career, try to contact persons in several different types of settings. Prepare a list of questions about the career and ask for advice on getting into that field.

If you find it difficult to locate individuals, you may be able to obtain some member names from the appropriate organization or association, such as the American Society of Agricultural Engineers. A local high school or college or your alma mater may be able to give you names of graduates who have gone into a particular field, and a library may have information on companies with the types of jobs you're interested in.

Individual accounts of a career must, however, be taken with a grain of salt. Every person has a unique work situation and personality. If, for example, the first forester you contact is completely negative about the job, don't give up on this career area immediately. Try to find out why this person doesn't like the career, but also contact several others in different settings to get their perspectives. After all, the experts on any one career area are those who are currently engaged in that particular line of work.

Women and Outdoor Careers

Adequately covering the topic of women in outdoor careers is beyond the scope of this book, but it is a subject that cannot be ignored. While greater numbers of women are entering fields traditionally dominated by men and are represented in virtually every occupation described in this book, women continue to be underrepresented in most outdoor careers. Many factors contribute to this imbalance.

Although women in other cultures, like those in our pioneer past, perform many physically challenging tasks, most women today are not being culturally prepared or encouraged to consider outdoor work. Some outdoor careers, such as commercial diving, require a great deal of physical strength and an irregular lifestyle that make them unattractive to many women. Additionally, many women do not have the high school grounding in mathematics and science needed for certain technical fields such as engineering.

A lack of female role models or mentors has also contributed to the smaller number of women in outdoor careers. Women seeking to enter a male-dominated career may find it helpful to locate a woman mentor for encouragement. If no one is available in your area, professional societies may provide names and addresses of women in occupations that interest you.

By the year 2000 women will make up virtually half of the labor force, according to *Fortune* magazine. While women may never be fully represented in all areas of outdoor work, it is important that they, as well as men, be encouraged to explore fully the careers that interest them and for which they believe they are suited.

A Final Word

Good luck as you explore your career options! Whether this is your first serious look for an appropriate career or you are considering a career change, the more knowledge you bring to your choice, the better your final decision will be.

Resources

The following organizations have seasonal as well as full-time positions.

Appalachian Mountain Club, Five Joy Street, Boston, MA 02108 (617-523-0636).

National Outdoor Leadership School, P.O. Box AA, Lander, WY 82520 (307-332-6973).

Outward Bound USA, 384 Field Point Road, Greenwich, CT 06830 (203-661-0797).

Student Conservation Association, Inc., P.O. Box 550, Charlestown, NH 03603-0550.

"**S**uccessful careers seldom happen by chance. With very few exceptions people who really get what they want in a career do so because they define clear objectives, develop plans and schedules for achieving their objectives, assume personal responsibility for implementing and following these plans, monitor their progress regularly, improve their plans when they aren't getting the desired results, and persevere in the face of frequent setbacks until their objectives are achieved."

Nicholas Weiler, *Reality and Career Planning*

Choosing Your Career

People choose careers in various ways. Some simply accept any position that is available and looks interesting. Others take a job because they know someone who does that type of work or works for the same organization. Still others take time for some self-assessment to discover who they are and what they can and want to do. They then research to learn what kinds of careers fit the type of person they are.

The fact that you have picked up this book probably means that you fall into this last category. Because many careers require extensive training, it is wise to research carefully before making your choice. Even if you are quite certain which career you wish to enter, take a little time to be sure you are headed in the best possible direction for the unique person that you are.

One of the first steps in choosing a career is to do a personal inventory. This will help you learn who you are and what you want to do. Important components are your interests, skills, and values.

You chose to read this book because the outdoors is important to you. What you need to decide is what role the outdoors should play in your career. Do you want to work outdoors, deal with a subject matter that relates to the outdoors, work for an organization that has outdoor concerns, or a combination of these? Consider these options as you continue to read this book.

Interests

Your interests are a key factor in career decision making. It is important to select a field in which you will be working on issues, content, or subject matter of interest to you. It is much more pleasant to spend thirty-five to forty hours a week or more working with a topic that greatly interests you than with something that bores you. Being aware of your interests can help you identify potential work environments and employers.

As you work through the following exercises picking out your skills and values, use interest as a criterion to keep or eliminate items from your list. For example, although you may be skilled at drawing, you may not like to do it. Picking a career that uses a skill that doesn't interest you would be counterproductive—you would not really enjoy that career.

Skills

When you examine different careers, one important thing to know is whether your skills match those required. A skill is generally defined as something you do well. Some of your skills may come to mind immediately. But because we aren't always tuned in to the things we do well, it is a good idea to spend some time assessing your skills.

Some of the skills you should consider are listed below; as you read through them, write down those that apply to you. Consider skills you have used in clubs, extracurricular activities, or hobbies, as well as on a job or in school.

administer	calculate
analyze	coach
arrange	coordinate
assemble	counsel
build	create

delegate

design

dramatize

edit

evaluate

explain

formulate

fund-raise

guide

interpret

interview

investigate

keep records

listen

manage

measure

mediate

negotiate

observe

organize

persuade

plan

predict

print

promote

question

recruit

repair

research

sell

sketch

speak publicly

supervise

talk

teach

translate

troubleshoot

write

This list is by no means exhaustive, and you will want to add other skills that may occur to you. As you write down the skills, it is helpful to add an example of a situation when you used each one. For example, you might note under "keep records" that as a 4-H club treasurer for three years, you kept accurate records of the membership dues and special sales projects.

Values

Also important to consider when making a career choice are your values. Values are those things that are most important to you. They provide satisfaction and add purpose and fulfillment to life. Often people do not realize that their values do not match those of their chosen profession until they are well into a career. Figuring out this part of the career match before other choices are made can help you avoid problems later on.

Read the following list and write down the values that are important to you.

achievement: perform important roles and be involved in momentous endeavors

autonomy: be free to work with little supervision and set my own schedule and priorities

distinction: be well known, be seen as successful, and have recognition and status in my chosen field

expertise: become a respected and trusted expert in my field

friendship: like and be liked by the people I work with

leadership: be an influential and respected leader

location: be able to live and work in the places I choose

pleasure: find enjoyment and have fun doing my work

power: be able to approve or disapprove different courses of action, make assignments, and control allocations and outcomes

security: obtain a secure and stable position

self-realization: do work that is challenging and allows me to fully develop my talents

service: help people in need and contribute to the satisfaction of others

wealth: earn a great deal of money so that I can be financially independent

Jot down any other values that are important to you. At this stage of the decision-making process, it is helpful to write down as much information about yourself as possible.

Temperament and Personal Qualities

Take a few moments to examine your personality and temperament. Are you outgoing, patient, reflective, conscientious, responsible? Which are your traits that you like best and would like to use on the job? Write these down.

Summer, Part-Time, and Volunteer Work

Knowing your interests, skills, values, and personal qualities will help you make a better match as you investigate the careers in this book. Another aid in deciding on a career is to actually do the type of work that interests you. Many outdoor jobs are available on a summer, part-time, or volunteer basis. A careful search can land you a summer job in the type of setting you believe best matches your needs and desires.

You may also want to check into volunteer work related to the field you're considering. Many communities have agencies that seek to match volunteers with jobs, and these can help you in your search. With a little persistence, however, you should be able to arrange your own volunteer position.

Working in the setting of a career that interests you—or at least in one that is similar—can help you decide whether you really want to get into that type of work. And the contacts you make in your summer, part-time, or volunteer work can be invaluable to you later when you begin your job search.

Additional Career Search Resources

At this point you may not yet be certain about the exact career that appeals to you and want to do some additional searching. Don't despair! Sometimes it simply takes a while to settle on a career. It is worth doing background research before you spend a lot of time and money preparing for a particular career. Help is as close as your public library, bookstore, or telephone.

You may wish to consult some of the excellent books that go into career selection in some depth. Or you might decide that you want assistance from a career counselor in identifying your interests, skills, and values; locating resources to explore different career options; or preparing for the job search. A career counselor can help you by providing an objective eye; it is often difficult to see yourself clearly. Counselors are also helpful in guiding you through the self-evaluation process if you get stuck.

Career counselors can be located fairly easily. One place to look is at nearby colleges and universities, most of which offer career counseling to their students. Many extend free use of this service to their graduates, and some also serve the public, although they often charge a fee. Nonprofit organizations, government agencies, and employment centers also offer career counseling, usually at little or no cost.

Private career counselors are usually quite good, although their fees will be higher, and many people find this type of counseling the most helpful. These counselors can be located in the yellow pages or through friends and relatives.

Before you invest too much time or money, make certain the counselor will be helpful to you. Arrange for a fifteen-minute free visit to see whether you feel comfortable with him or her. A good personality match is important. Also find out whether the counselor is a Nationally Certified Career Counselor, shown by the acronym NCCC following his or her name. This certification indicates professional recognition, a commitment to continuing education, the passing of two national exams, recommendations from the field, and supervised experiences.

You may choose to consult one of the excellent books that give in-depth assistance in making career decisions. The books recommended here should be available in libraries or bookstores.

Resources

Anderson, Nancy. *Work with Passion.* New York: Carroll & Graf Publishers, 1984.

Benjamin, Janice, and Barbara Block. *How to Be Happily Employed in Washington, D.C.* New York: Random House, 1990. Other editions of this book for Boston, Dallas–Fort Worth and San Francisco contain the same useful introductory material on the career search.

Bolles, Richard Nelson. *What Color Is Your Parachute? A Practical Manual for Job-Hunters & Career Changers.* Berkeley, CA: Ten Speed Press. This classic in the field is updated annually.

Figler, Howard E. *The Complete Job-Search Handbook,* revised and expanded. New York: Henry Holt and Company, 1988.

———. *PATH: A Career Workbook for Liberal Arts Students.* Cranston, RI: Carroll Press, 1979. A classic.

Krannich, Ronald L. *Careering and Re-careering for the 1990s.* Manassas, VA: Impact Publications, 1989.

Weiler, Nicholas W. *Reality and Career Planning: A Guide for Personal Growth.* Reading, MA: Addison-Wesley Publishing Company, 1977. A classic.

Yeager, Neil M. *Career Map.* New York: John Wiley & Sons, 1988.

2

"And he gave it for his opinion, that whoever could make two ears of corn, or two blades of grass, to grow upon a spot of ground where only one grew before, would deserve better of mankind, and do more essential service to his country, than the whole race of politicians put together."

Jonathan Swift

Agriculture and Food Production

Farming, one of the oldest of outdoor occupations, is an appropriate place to begin an examination of outdoor careers. When the United States was settled by European immigrants, the small farm was one means of "taming" the wilderness. The land was cleared, plowed, planted, and harvested. As the country grew, the government encouraged this type of development through land grant policies, homesteading acts, and the sale of land at low cost. As a result, the U.S. farm economy is based on the family farm unit in which the farmer owns or rents land and manages the total resource.

With the advent of machinery to aid in harvesting, such as the cotton gin and the harvester, many farms in the nineteenth century grew beyond the scope of the small family farm into plantations or large farms specializing in one crop, such as cotton, tobacco, wheat, or sugar beets.

As farming has become more efficient in the United States, a smaller number of the total labor force is employed in the field. Less than 7 percent of the U.S. population produces enough to feed the entire country and to make it a world leader in agriculture and the largest exporter of farm products.

One prominent trend in U.S. agriculture has been a decline in the number of individual farm operations as these have been combined by either purchase or lease. Between 1935 and 1970, the number of farm units decreased by almost half. In spite of this trend toward ever larger farms, other types of farms can be successfully and profitably operated.

This chapter examines careers related to the various types of farming, agriculture, and food production. It also suggests alternate methods of organizing a farming operation through two profiles of persons who have successfully bucked the agricultural trend toward large enterprises.

Agronomy

Salary Range: starting between $16,000 and $19,800
Educational Requirements: college
Employment Outlook: good

Agronomy relates to the scientific aspects of crop production by studying plants and soils and the surrounding environment. The two main areas within agronomy are crop science and soil science.

Crop science looks at production of quality seed that will yield larger crops of higher value. In the process it examines details such as genetics, cellular biology and molecular genetics, breeding, physiology, and managing field and turf crops. Crops that are considered include alfalfa, corn, cotton, peanuts, rice, soybeans, sunflowers, turf grass, and wheat.

Soil science examines the soils as they relate to growing plants. The physics, chemistry, origin, microbiology, mineralogy, fertility, and management of the soil are all probed. Soil science also looks at other aspects of soil uses, such as reclamation, waste disposal, building foundations and road construction, and waterways.

A challenging field, agronomy offers an opportunity to use science to help increase the supply of quality crops while working to protect and preserve the environment. American agriculture is very productive, and there are no great concerns about the quantity or quality of food. The challenge to agronomists, however, is to meet food shortage problems around the world by helping areas with limited food production resources to use them more efficiently.

Agronomic research is highly technical, requiring very specific training and the use of some research tools such as computers, scanning electron microscopes, radioisotope detectors, satellites, and telemetry units. Use of these tools involves a creative imagination and acute observational skills. Knowledge of both physical sciences (chemistry, physics, and mathematics) and natural sciences (biology and geology) may be required to solve problems agronomists tackle. Other scientists with whom agronomists may work closely include biochemists, microbiologists, entomologists, geneticists, plant pathologists, and agricultural economists and engineers.

Genetic engineering is a new field within agronomy that seeks to improve plants by transferring desirable genes. Plants that are more insect or disease resistant may be developed, or the amino acid content may be improved to make the product more nutritious. This is a team-oriented field that offers great challenges.

Course background for agronomists is heavy in the sciences, including biology, chemistry, mathematics, physics, geology, botany, and microbiology. Applied science courses in areas such as genetics, plant pathology, soil chemistry, plant physiology, and biochemistry will also assist in preparation for an agronomy career.

Agronomists work in varied settings. Some are educators who teach and work with college students, informing them and seeking to interest them in further studies in agronomy. Extension agronomists also work with people; farmers and other groups who face problems often contact agricultural extension services, which are located at land grant colleges. Agronomists may also serve an educational and service function in industry by sharing their detailed knowledge about a company's services or products.

The Soil Conservation and Forest services provide government employment for many agronomists. Urban projects such as zoning, parks, land-use planning, and highway landscaping increasingly involve agronomists. Agronomic job opportunities overseas are available through government programs, aid groups, and philanthropic foundations, as well as large agricultural industries.

Other types of work in agronomy include research in industry, sales of agricultural products, and professional consulting services. Many people who have studied agronomy become farmers or ranchers and use their training to produce food or fiber crops. Agronomists also work as farm managers, bank loan specialists, and superintendents of golf courses or forests, as well as in top administrative positions in industry.

See Profile, page 29.

Beekeeping (Apiculture)

Salary Range: varies tremendously
Educational Requirements: self-study or on-the-job training
Employment Outlook: fair

Beekeepers' work involves gathering honey and placing bees where their pollination will directly benefit farmers. A beekeeper will make certain a hive is in good repair, the colony and queen bee are healthy and flourishing, and the bees have enough food to maintain themselves. A great deal of the work is done outdoors except for some maintenance tasks and record keeping.

Experience, gained from working with a beekeeper or by investing in a few hives, is all that is necessary to get into this career. Persons interested in commercial beekeeping will want to consider some schooling, either a two- or a four-year program with some apiculture courses.

Beekeepers are mainly hobbyists or part-time workers; only a small number do commercial work. Some raise bees to sell, and as the number of bee hobbyists increases, this option may offer more possibilities.

Those with a bachelor's degree and experience may find work as state inspectors. A doctorate is needed to qualify for research with the U.S. Department of Agriculture or a university. Some areas of research include problems facing bees, the nectar and pollen yields of plants, and the content of honey. College teaching and working for a commercial bee firm are other options for apiculturists.

Farm Management

Salary Range: from $19,500 to $48,600, depending on the size and number of operations managed

Educational Requirements: college plus continuing education

Employment Outlook: good, but competition for positions is keen

A farm manager is a person who operates farms owned by others; one manager may be in charge of as many as thirty-five units at one time. This position requires knowledge of both agricultural practices and business methods. Exact duties vary according to the size and type of farm managed and the amount of authority delegated by the owner.

A manager's duties involve organizing and administering farm work; determining labor needs; and hiring, supervising, and, when necessary, firing employees. The farm manager organizes schedules for planting, harvesting, and marketing. He or she determines land use and which agricultural methods would be best. Other functions of the farm manager may include the purchase of supplies and equipment, the maintenance and upkeep of equipment and buildings, the care and feeding of livestock, and some marketing and accounting.

Work for the farm manager involves much walking and outdoor duties. At times the job may involve operating farm equipment. Traveling between farms managed and to the office is also necessary. Hours at work vary according to the season; during busy periods the manager often must work more than eight hours a day.

A farm manager should be able to work well with others, as he or she will be both answering to the owner and supervising workers. Other requirements are the ability to objectively evaluate new developments, techniques, and machinery, and to do detailed planning.

Good background for farm management is involvement in a 4-H club or the Future Farmers of America to gain both training and experience. A bachelor of science degree in an area related to agriculture that includes courses in agricultural economics, business, agronomy, animal science, and other subjects will be helpful. Some continuing professional education will help the employed manager keep abreast of new methods and procedures.

Opportunities in this field are limited because of an overall decline in the industry. Competition for available jobs will be intense, and the edge will go to individuals with specialized training and good experience or agricultural background. Professional farm managers may be hired by a commercial bank or an independent farm-management firm, or they may be self-employed.

Farming

Salary Range: varies tremendously depending on type of farm and weather conditions

Educational Requirements: none, although college is an asset

Employment Outlook: poor

There are a variety of types of farms, generally categorized by product. In almost none of them is growth expected, largely because of the trend toward consolidation of farmlands into larger-sized farms. With the exception of dairy, livestock, and poultry farms, which are run year-round, much of the work is highly seasonal. Farmers often work elsewhere during the off-season to supplement their incomes. Following are basic descriptions of the types of farming. Dairy farming, though not a growth area, may be easier to get into than the others.

Cotton, Tobacco, and Peanut: Cotton, tobacco, and peanuts are among the major crops grown. Usually a farmer grows only one of them because they require very different farming methods.

Grain: Grains grown include corn, wheat, rye, and grain sorghums, which are used as food for people or for animals. Although grain production is increasing, this is mainly because of improved farming methods that enable bigger crops to be raised on fewer acres.

Dairy: The major dairy-farming products are cows, which are bred and raised, and milk, which is supplied to the milk and milk-products industries. Unlike most types of farms, these provide a year-round income. Many dairy farmers also grow crops as feed for their herds.

Livestock: The major types of livestock raised for profit—cattle, hogs, sheep, and goats—are raised for food or for their hides or hair. Other livestock farmers raise horses, mules, or donkeys as draft animals to pull heavy loads. Some farmers raise only one type of animal, but others raise a number of different types and also grow the crops to feed them.

Poultry: Chickens, turkeys, and ducks are raised on poultry farms, which usually specialize in one type of production, such as meat, eggs, or breeding.

Fruit: Fruits grown and marketed for profit include citrus varieties, apples, pears, peaches, berries, melons, nuts, and grapes.

Vegetable: Some of the vegetables raised for profit are beans, potatoes, corn, carrots, tomatoes, lettuce, and peppers. The size of vegetable farms and the methods of marketing vary from small farms with roadside stands to farms larger than 150 acres that employ field hands.

See Profiles, pages 32 and 36.

Herb Growing and Marketing

Salary Range: varies tremendously

Educational Requirements: none, although college is an asset

Employment Outlook: uncertain; this is a developing field

Herb growing and marketing is a fairly new field that is becoming more important as herb use increases. Herb businesses are usually small or medium-sized home-based businesses, often involving only the owner or less than five employees.

According to Maureen Buehrle, executive director of the International Herb Growers & Marketers Association, most people go into herb growing "from a hobby that becomes overwhelming. There is very little in the way of education available, but a solid background in farming seems to help. Also, because of the wide variety of species involved, some knowledge of taxonomy is becoming extremely important." She says that knowledge of marketing is also helpful, "because commercial herb production is relatively new and the markets are not readily defined."

Those interested in pursuing this career should contact some of the existing organizations or networks. Through these you can gain valuable contacts and information from newsletters and association meetings.

Range Management

Salary Range: starting between $13,000 and $16,200; average $28,000 with experience
Educational Requirements: college
Employment Outlook: fair; growth in this small field depends on federal funding of agencies and projects

Rangelands constitute about 45 percent of the world's land. This broad category includes natural grasslands, shrub communities, forests, savannas, tundra, wetlands, alpine communities, and most deserts. The basic means of food production from rangeland is through livestock grazing.

Only in the last fifty years has range management become a specific discipline. It takes into account ecology and ways to manage the range ecosystems to yield desired products in a natural and economical manner. Rangeland specialists deal with everything that affects the range: soil, water, plants, animals, and climate. Much of the work throughout the year will be done out on the range in all types of weather, but range specialists also spend time in the office keeping records. Some may be college teachers and may do research as well.

Required education is a bachelor of science degree in a major such as range science, range management, or range ecology. Basic required courses are botany, biology, chemistry, math, statistics, English, and public speaking. Specialized courses are genetics, ecology, climate, biochemistry, soil science, animal science and nutrition, plant taxonomy, physiology, and geology.

Another important skill for range managers is public relations. They must work with people and earn their trust, whether they are handing down government rulings or dealing with ranchers, oil workers, hunters and fishers, or government workers. They may also need to work in cooperation with specialists in areas such as wildlife, hydrology, forestry, soils, and recreation.

Most jobs for rangeland specialists are in different federal government departments. Some jobs also exist in state and local governments and in private firms. Range management is a good major for people who plan to become ranchers. The number of jobs in this area is likely to remain constant; jobs will open up mainly through attrition.

Rural Appraisal

Salary Range: starting between $13,000 and $17,300; average $27,000 with experience; experienced self-employed from $37,800 to $48,700

Educational Requirements: college plus license and continuing education.

Employment Outlook: good in states with rural properties; competition for positions is keen

A rural appraiser estimates the value of rural real estate. Appraisals are needed to provide the market value of a property in order to determine taxes, selling price, rental payments, the legal distribution of property among persons, or the assets of individuals, firms, or corporations.

The appraiser must collect and interpret data on the property, such as the condition and maintenance; the type of rent or ownership; and the cost of real estate taxes, insurance, maintenance, services, and other expenses.

Appraisers must travel to property sites to inspect and examine them. This involves measuring and walking throughout each property to evaluate it. A major part of the work is done in the office, studying collected data, writing reports, and maintaining records.

Rural appraisers need to learn about land values and economic conditions and should have an agricultural degree with courses in real estate, business, economics, and journalism. Because some states require licensing, continuing education is necessary. Important personal characteristics include honesty, integrity, and tact, as well as accuracy, attention to detail, good oral and written communications skills, and the ability to interpret data.

Earnings of rural appraisers vary considerably, depending especially on experience, training, and the geographic location. Some rural appraisers are employed by federal and state agencies and insurance companies, and others are self-employed. Hours may be irregular, ranging from less than twenty-five to more than fifty hours a week.

The demand for rural appraisers is higher in the West, where there is a larger amount of rural property. The number of jobs is expected to remain constant, as workers are needed to replace those who retire or leave the career. Competition for available positions is expected to be keen, and the edge will go to well-trained and experienced individuals.

Resources
General
Higher Education Programs in the U.S. Department of Agriculture (pamphlet), Director, Higher Education Programs, Rm. 350-1, Admin. Bldg., U.S. Department of Agriculture, Washington, DC 20250.
101 Paths to Success! and *Energize the Green Machine* (pamphlets),

Purdue University, School of Agriculture, West Lafayette, IN 47907.

21st Century Explorers: The Science of Agriculture (pamphlet), Ag in the Classroom, 234-W, USDA, Washington, DC 20250.

Employment Opportunities for College Graduates in the Food and Agricultural Sciences: Agriculture, Natural Resources, and Veterinary Medicine (pamphlet), Higher Education Programs, Office of Grants and Program Systems, U.S. Department of Agriculture, Washington, DC 20250.

Agriculture
Economic Research Division, American Farm Bureau Federation, 225 Touhy Avenue, Park Ridge, IL 60068.

Agronomy, Crops, and Soils
American Society of Agronomy/Crop Science Society of America/Soil Science Society of America, 677 South Segoe Road, Madison, WI 53711.

Beekeeping
The American Beekeeping Federation, Inc., P.O. Box 1038, Jessup, GA 31545.

Farm Management and Rural Appraisal
American Society of Farm Managers and Rural Appraisers, 950 South Cherry Street, Suite 106, Denver, CO 80222-2662.

Herb Growing
International Herb Growers & Marketers Association, P.O. Box 281, Silver Springs, PA 17575.

The Herbal Connection, 3343 Nolt Road, Lancaster, PA 17601 (717-898-3017)

Organic Farming and Community Support Agriculture
Sylvia and Walter Ehrhardt, 1032 Hoffmaster Road, Knoxville, MD 21758 (301-834-9247).

Range Management

Careers in Range Science and Range Management (pamphlet),
Society for Range Management, 1839 York Street, Denver, CO
80206.

Soil Scientist
Karen Kotlar

"I've always liked science and the outdoors, and this career mixes these two very well. I'm also very concerned with the environment and, ultimately, with feeding people." Karen Kotlar describes soil science as a very sensible, understandable science that is essential to food production and wise land use.

Kotlar has a bachelor of science degree in agronomy and international agriculture and a master's in agronomy and natural resources. Except for her international agriculture emphasis, which she used as a springboard into a stint with the Peace Corps, Kotlar says this is probably a typical background for agronomists working in soil science.

For the past ten years Kotlar has been a soil survey party leader with the U.S. Department of Agriculture Soil Conservation Service in different areas of New York, most recently in Utica. To map the soils of the United States, a task that is almost completed, soil scientists classify the soil based on a system of soil taxonomy—a thorough and unique classification system. During mapping season—mid-April to the end of October—Kotlar spends most of her time in the field.

On a typical mapping day Kotlar arrives at the office early to examine aerial photographs of the area she plans to cover with a stereoscope, an instrument that gives a three-dimensional picture of the landscape. Then she goes into the field, chooses an area to transect, sets a compass bearing, and digs holes at places in the landscape where there are distinctive features such as moisture, vegetation, topography, or soil color. Then she logs what she finds.

"I do what we call a profile description," she explains. "That means I describe the layers of soil from the surface to six feet down. I detail the horizons, color, texture, structure, composition, types of roots, and rock fragments. After making this description I make as precise a classification as possible."

"In my job a true enjoyment of the outdoors is essential,"

Kotlar declares. "I deal with problems such as inclement weather, bothersome bugs, thorny bushes, and mucky soils." Outdoor skills such as orienteering are essential.

An ability to work independently and make decisions on her own are also important in her job, according to Kotlar. "Not all of the decisions are clear-cut. This is more of a conceptual than an exact science." In other words, soils present a range of characteristics rather than one single composite profile. The combination of these characteristics defines a concept that a soil in a particular spot in the landscape represents. Although Kotlar enjoys this aspect of her job, she says it can get tiring. Some people skills are also necessary when Kotlar must work on private property. Although most landowners are very cooperative, confrontations with irate property owners do occur; diplomacy is essential in dealing with them. While such disputes don't happen often, dealing with them alone can be a challenge for a woman. "Soil science is a male-dominated field, and I've gotten used to being one of the few women soil scientists in the state," she says matter-of-factly.

"I love the independence of my work," Kotlar affirms. "I construct my own day and make my own plans. I may walk over ten different landscapes in a day. There are a lot of surprises. I may find an incredibly beautiful place or see unexpected wildlife. I don't always know what I'm going to find."

Her work also contributes to an important end. "I am assisting in the conservation of the soil, and that is important to me. I hope that people will be wiser in their use of the land." Kotlar also enjoys the other scientists with whom she comes in contact—"people with an earth-bondedness, a healthiness, and a true appreciation of the outdoors."

Because the United States is almost completely mapped, jobs like Kotlar's are not plentiful; future jobs for soil scientists will take on different forms. Soil scientist jobs in the future will include working with planning boards, assessors, and land users who will apply information about the soil. New consultant companies will also need the skills of soil scientists.

Kotlar says, "It really is hard to be a field soil scientist for your whole life. In a typical career you may advance to other levels of management or administration." She is currently in the process of moving on to a position as a resource inventory specialist. In this position with the Soil Conservation Service, she will oversee the National Resource Inventory Program, which monitors trends in changing land use in New York state.

"There will always be jobs for conservationists with a soil background," Kotlar declares. She advises persons interested in this career not to limit themselves strictly to soil conservation: "Don't be tunnel-visioned. Learn about other natural resources and prepare for possible management work. Stay current in your information and keep broadening your skills. Knowledge of the soil resource base is essential for conservation and resource management work, and with this you can go in a lot of different directions."

See Agronomy, page 18.

Dairy Farmer
Valentine Yutzy

"You don't have to get big to get good," dairy farmer Valentine Yutzy says emphatically. "In my opinion, no farm or factory should be allowed to operate until it reduces waste to the lowest common denominator."

Yutzy is out of sync with conventional ideas about farming in the midwestern United States. A farmer since 1963, Yutzy and his wife, Anne, have farmed the 240-acre Kramer Homestead in Plain City, Ohio, since 1972. Three families are currently supported by the farm, which according to conventional wisdom is too small to maintain that many people. In fact, the farm has been so profitable that the families annually divide between $18,000 and $20,000 in bonuses and also defer income to reduce taxes.

Yutzy, who was recently named Ohio State Conservationist of the Year and listed as one of the top ten conservationists in the nation, practices what is known in agronomy as a *closed system*. Yutzy explains what this means: "We try to raise all the feed needed for our livestock, and we also try to feed all the grain and forage that we raise. We then use our waste products [manure and crop residue] as our primary nutrients for future crops. In other words, we try to balance our agronomy and animal husbandry enterprises and do most of our marketing in milk and meat. We try to get these two enterprises to complement each other so that we need to buy very few outside inputs for our farming operation. We process our own soybeans for protein and energy [fat] supplementation of feed rations."

Yutzy practices conservation in four major areas: water-quality enhancement (by preventing nonfiltered surface runoff into streams); improvement of soil life and tilth (the part of the surface soil affected by tillage); prevention of soil erosion; and energy conservation. "One of the things we have been able to achieve," Yutzy reports, "is that our amount of electrical use in 1989 was almost identical to that of 1969, yet our farm has had normal expansion."

Although he hadn't finished high school, Yutzy spent two years in college as a premed student in the early 1960s. He was accepted by the medical school at Ohio State University, but with three young children, he chose instead to go into farming in 1963. Yutzy says that the science courses he took during those two years provided him with a foundation in the natural sciences.

He has since studied agronomy, but Yutzy does not call himself an agronomist. "A farmer needs to be a 'jack of many trades' and also a master of as many as possible," Yutzy says. "Or, in other words, I need to be a generalist to see all the parts of the whole and also a specialist to be able to expertly function in one part." Yutzy is also self-trained in ecology, engineering ("building design, heating and ventilation, and electrical and mechanical applications"), marketing, and animal husbandry.

Yutzy farms in partnership with his two sons, and the three families hire very little outside help. They do most of their own building and repair work as well as any necessary mechanical and electrical work.

Personable and an easy conversationalist, Yutzy is adamant that size does not determine quality. "Free-enterprise business courses generally teach that if you are not growing, then you are going backward. On the contrary, I think that quality must always supersede quantity." He adds, "We here in America have moved toward bigness as a sign of individual success, to the long-term detriment of ecology and opportunity."

Yutzy's farming philosophy builds on his own personal philosophy. "I believe that we are stewards of what God has given us," he says with quiet conviction. "If we become possessors of it, we handle things in a much different way than if we are stewards of it, handling it for somebody else. When we are possessors of it, we can be too willing to take a risk, we think too highly of our own abilities, and we want to make a quick dollar. What we really need to do is to handle it and pass it on to the next generation in as good or better shape than it was when we got it."

Yutzy has this advice for those who want to get into dairy farming: "If you want to have fifty cows, get twenty-five heifer calves in April and start feeding them. That's not a big expense. Get another twenty-five two months later, and do the same the next year. You will cull better than 50 percent, but you won't have nearly the expense if you raise them yourself as if you buy them all ready to milk. You will also learn if you can raise your own replacements, which you need to do to have a successful dairy. So start out by being sure that you can raise your own replacements. When they are two years old, start milking in a stanchion barn where you walk in among the animals. That way you learn to know the animals and how to be responsive to their needs. Then you can move into a parlor where you aren't closely associated with the animals, if that's what you want to do."

"One of my philosophies," Yutzy relates with a chuckle, "is that you make more money thinking than you do working." As the senior farm operator, he usually spends several hours on the telephone each morning doing business and planning the general running of the farm. "My time outside varies," he says. "Sometimes I spend all day outside doing physical work and sometimes I'm out very little." A computer is very useful in farm operation. It provides accessible information and has a program to formulate the mix of corn, soybeans, and other ingredients for the animals' feed. The computer doesn't necessarily save time, however; Yutzy spends at least an hour a day keeping it up-to-date.

Yutzy is optimistic about the future of farming. "No matter what else happens in the world, people will still have to have food. I think we need a different emphasis in what we produce so that we produce quality first and then quantity." In fact, he predicts that this is the future for agriculture: "By the year 2000, quality is going to be much more in demand. I don't see anything but a good future for the farmer who is capable of working with the laws of nature and the biological aspect of farming."

See Farming, page 22.

Organic Farmers
Sylvia and Walter Ehrhardt

For organic farmers Sylvia and Walter Ehrhardt, it all began when they read the book *Living the Good Life,* by Helen and Scott Nearing. The Nearings wrote about their move to the country after they realized that they wanted more from life than living and working in the city. "When I read of the pleasure they experienced living near the earth, watching the seasons change, and growing their own vegetables, something resonated very deep within me," Sylvia relates.

At that time, in 1972, the Ehrhardts lived and worked in Washington, D.C. Deciding to change their lives, they began taking agriculture courses and exploring their options. In late 1979 Sylvia left her public relations job in the Carter White House, and they moved to Knoxville, Maryland, just across the Potomac from Harper's Ferry, West Virginia.

Their whole seventy-six-acre tract was in trees, so their initial challenge was to clear land. Then they planted strawberries, blackberries, red raspberries, and miniature squash. By 1981 they were supplying restaurants as far away as Washington, D.C. Walter initially kept his position in the Department of Housing and Urban Development on a part-time basis. He quit altogether in 1986.

"We wanted to create our own environment," says Sylvia of their move. "When we cleared land to build our home, we took out only the trees we wanted out." Over the years they have continued to clear land at the rate of a half acre a year.

They also began to change the emphasis of their farm. In 1987 they spoke to a group of chemically sensitive people, who asked if the Ehrhardts could provide them with organically grown vegetables. All of the agriculture courses Sylvia was taking were chemical oriented, and when she inquired she was told it was not possible to farm organically. So they began to attend conferences and workshops and joined an organic growers association. "We did lots of research and reading," she explains, "and then we learned through trial and error."

By 1990 they began a "pick your own" operation—people came to the farm to pick berries—although they still supplied a few local restaurants. They then changed the major focus of the farm to community support agriculture, a Japanese style of farming that brings consumers and growers together.

Sylvia explains: "People buy shares, at $360 for a full share for twenty weeks. In return we provide enough in-season vegetables, herbs, and berries to serve two to four persons weekly. We pack quantities in one- to two-quart containers and put everything into shopping bags, and people come by once a week to pick up their food." They now support the equivalent of fifty-three families (some have bought half shares).

The Ehrhardts' daughter manages the farm, and both Sylvia and Walter work there. Additionally, they usually have two interns who work four hours a day in exchange for room and board and information about organic farming. Occasionally the Ehrhardts also hire neighbors to help with the harvest.

As their knowledge and practice of organic farming has grown, their work has also changed, Sylvia says. "We now give workshops and have groups coming to look at our operation. We're starting to use the farm as an organic-farming demonstration and training center."

Sylvia is enthusiastic about community support agriculture. "It is one of the most exciting concepts I've come across. It cuts out the middleman and does not cost as much as a co-op. It provides an equitable amount for everyone. We figured out last year that each person who paid $360 received $600 worth of food."

"The small farmer needs to know about this concept," she continues. "You do not have to be big and own heavy equipment to succeed in farming. One acre, if planted intensively, can grow enough food for twenty-five people. And farmers certainly do not have to farm organically in order to operate this way."

The Ehrhardts have found that other countries are also interested in this concept. In fact, they took a trip to eastern

Europe in the fall of 1991 to talk about their experiences. "We have a small acreage and we are living from this," explains Sylvia. "A lot of people want to know about it."

The major bonus for the Ehrhardts is the lifestyle, but they are making a profit as well. "If we wanted to make lots of money, we would expand the acres we are farming," Sylvia explains. "As it is, we have our own honey—we have six hives— and our own food to freeze and process."

She says that she is very happy they made this change in lifestyle. "I only wish I had done it earlier. Living near nature this way is much more sane. I like the city and many things about the city. Now we can combine the best of the city and the country so that we really do have a good life."

See Farming, page 22.

"The universe is full of magical things patiently waiting for our wits to grow sharper."

Eden Phillpots

Biological Sciences

Biology, the study of living things and their life processes, is commonly known as the life sciences. Life scientists are interested in the beginnings and the protection of all forms of life, from the tiniest cell to the largest animal.

The biological sciences may be approached as either basic or applied sciences. Persons who work in basic biology are mainly interested in the study of living things. In contrast, applied biologists look for knowledge that will improve the world; for example, they may work in agriculture to improve crop production.

The field of biology contains many broad disciplines, with opportunities for specialization in each one. They include aquatic biology, the study of plants and animals that live in water; botany, the study of plants; ecology, the study of the relationship of organisms to environment; mycology, the study of fungi; taxonomy, the study of the genetic relationship among species; and zoology, or animal biology, the study of animals. The related field of veterinary medicine will also be covered in this chapter.

Biologists work in widely varied settings. By far the largest number work in institutions of higher learning. They are not all teachers, however; research and laboratory positions are also available at universities and colleges. Many biologists work for private business or industry in positions involving research, testing, product improvement, and sales. Biologists at colleges and universities may also be employed by industries as special consultants.

Governments at all levels—federal, state, and municipal—employ almost a quarter of biology graduates. These job settings include national parks and monuments, agricultural research stations, and museums. A smaller percentage of biologists work for nonprofit organizations.

Aquatic Biology

Salary Range: varies widely depending on education, experience, location, and type of job; beginning rates for master's degree holders from $19,400 to $29,200; for those with a doctorate, $29,200 to $35,600; for persons with experience, about $41,200; very experienced persons in senior positions, $57,300

Educational Requirements: college

Employment Outlook: uncertain; better with an advanced degree

An aquatic biologist studies plants and animals that live in a freshwater ecosystem. (The saltwater equivalent is a marine biologist.) The basic academic background necessary for an aquatic biologist is a bachelor's degree in biological sciences, as it is difficult to pick up the knowledge needed through work alone. The course load should emphasize the natural sciences and should also be strong in the physical sciences.

A bachelor's degree qualifies a candidate for an introductory job, while some additional experience or a master's degree is necessary for an intermediate job. Advanced jobs will go to candidates with a doctorate or substantial experience.

Positions in aquatic biology are among the first to be cut in a financial squeeze; this is the situation governments faced in the early 1990s. Since environmental problems are of great concern, private companies will continue to expand to fill the gaps left by government cutbacks, and specialization in the field will open additional positions. Two areas of specialization are effluent toxicity testing and hydraulics, which involves quantifying the amount of water needed in a fish habitat and timing releases from a dam.

See Profile, page 53.

Botany

Salary Range: depends on education, experience, location, and type of job; beginning rates for master's degree holders from $21,600 to $27,000; for those with a doctorate, $30,200 to $41,100; for experienced botanists, $59,400 to $70,300

Educational Requirements: bachelor's degree at the minimum

Employment Outlook: good, especially for those with a doctorate, because of environmental and food supply concerns

Botany is the study of plants, from tiny organisms to giant trees. The variety of fields in botany is enormous, and the work settings are diverse. Botanists include many kinds of plant biologists and interrelated specialties. The specialties and varied career opportunities within the field are attractive features of the plant sciences.

Work settings include universities and research institutes. The U.S. Agricultural Research Service (ARS), part of the Department of Agriculture, is one government department that hires plant scientists. Headquartered in Beltsville, Maryland, the ARS conducts research across the United States.

Careers in botany that have the greatest potential for outdoor work are plant taxonomy, plant exploration, plant pathology, and plant physiology. Botanists may also find outdoor work opportunities as resource managers in state heritage programs or by doing fieldwork.

Some areas of botany that have become separate disciplines are agronomy and forestry, which are covered in chapters 2 and 4.

Plant Taxonomy

Plant taxonomists identify and classify different plants. In their work they spend part of their time outdoors gathering information and part indoors examining the data gathered. Tropical rain forests, which contain many plant species not yet cataloged, are one location where a plant taxonomist may work to find new species. A new emphasis by the government on wetlands preservation has opened up other possible areas in which to work. This does not appear to be a field of great promise, but it is a specialty that will complement other work in botany.

Take the case of Dr. Pat Gladu, for example. A botany professor at a small liberal arts college in Kentucky, Gladu has a master's degree in botany with an emphasis in ecology and taxonomy and a doctorate in plant physiology. She worked one summer as a plant taxonomist consulting in wetlands evaluation in a job specifically related to legislation on preserving wetlands in the state of Maryland.

When people wanted to build homes on lands that had formerly been wetlands, Gladu explains, "I was called in by real estate agents and the planning commission to look at areas and determine whether or not they were viable wetlands." Additionally, the National Heritage Foundation contacted her to identify endangered plant species.

"Taxonomists get to travel a lot when they're doing research. That's wonderful," she says enthusiastically. "During the mild weather we do a lot of fieldwork collecting plants, and then we go back to our labs to research in the winter. If you can find someone to support you, you can make a life of it."

According to Gladu, a variety of employers hire plant taxonomists, although often these jobs are advertised for ecologists or environmentalists. One employer is the U.S. Army, which has hired persons to identify vegetation and learn how much damage has been caused by war games. Botanical gardens and institutions such as the Smithsonian Institution in Washington, D.C., also have some positions for taxonomists. One unusual position with a Texas oil company involved in exploration used the taxonomist's skill in identifying pollen grains. The type of pollen present was a possible indicator of whether they were close to oil.

With the continuation of environmental concerns such as the wetlands issue, there could be more opportunities in this type of work. But because, as Gladu says, "plant taxonomy is a very narrow area," it is difficult to tell if the field will expand.

Plant Exploration
Plant explorers are involved in searching out new species of plants.

Plants not yet studied and classified not only may be interesting as species, but they also may be very important for what they might contribute to life on our planet. A new food crop or drugs that can be used to cure or treat diseases may be discovered. Plants that are not yet classified might be used to aid in genetic engineering by contributing to the gene pool.

This is a field with potential, much of it not yet tapped, according to Dr. Steven King, vice president for ethnobotany and conservation at Shaman Pharmaceuticals. King says that many of the available positions are not actually titled plant explorer; the job titles include field researcher, international sourcing specialist, plant collector, and research ethnobotanist. People in these positions do not necessarily go into the jungle searching for plants; they may talk with native people in their search.

King indicates that there aren't a lot of full-time plant exploration positions. Most of the jobs that involve this type of work are with research institutes and academic institutions. Private agribusiness employers, such as Monsanto and Native Plants, Inc., have some positions, as do cosmetics and pharmaceutical companies; they are not major employers, however. Pharmaceutical companies often contract these positions out to workers in the country that is being explored.

"This is not a career that can be pigeonholed," says King. "As people realize the importance of native people's knowledge and the value of plants, this type of work will increase."

Plant Pathology
Plant pathologists are scientists whose specialty is plant health. To keep plants healthy, the plant pathologist must know about the organisms that cause diseases in plants and affect the growth, yield, or quality of the plant product. Plant pathologists must know the basics of several disciplines related to plant pathology, including biochemistry, botany, ecology, epidemiology, genetics, microbiology, and molecular biology, and physiology.

Plant pathologists work both in laboratories and in the field examining crops or diseased plants. They identify diseases and experiment with various treatments to find a cure. Sophisticated laboratory research usually involves the use of an electron micro-scope and computer technology. To control diseases, plant patholo-gists use biological, chemical, or cultural methods or perhaps a combination. Cooperation with other fields, such as organic chem-istry, is important in order to discover and develop new chemicals to control plant diseases.

Most plant pathologists major in one of the biological sciences for undergraduate study and then study plant pathology at the graduate level. Although some jobs are available for those with just a bachelor's degree, opportunities in research generally go to per-sons with graduate work.

Dr. Oscar Grybauskas teaches plant pathology in the Univer-sity of Maryland (College Park) botany department. He also does research and works with county cooperative extension depart-ments. "As a specialist, I support the needs of the county extension agents," Grybauskas explains. "I develop an education program for them as needed. I have contact with farmers and growers to ex-plain what is going on, and I do research. Plant pathology, after all, is driven by current problems."

According to Grybauskas, integrated pest management is a developing area. This encompasses the three pest categories for plants: plant pathology, entomology (study of insects), and weed sciences.

Four types of employers hire plant pathologists, says Gry-bauskas. Chemical and pesticide industries have a need for them. The government at the state and federal levels also has positions—for example, in regulating plant trade across state lines. The Envi-ronmental Protection Agency and the Department of Agriculture hire plant pathologists, as do universities. And a new area of em-ployment Grybauskus sees developing in this field is private con-sultant work.

The job market is fairly limited because both the government and universities face tight budgets. This means that the demand for private consultants to fill this void will likely increase. Gry-bauskas suggests that the larger agricultural states may have some positions for plant pathologists to work on problems facing the money crops, vegetables and fruit.

Plant Physiology

Plant physiologists are scientists who study the way plants work. The science of plant physiology is dependent upon experiments for its knowledge. Basic research in plant physiology is simply an attempt to find answers—no benefit is necessary from the quest. Applied research, however, involves trying to solve problems faced in agriculture, forestry, or range management. The end result is to provide plants with the desired appearance that give the highest yield with the best nutritional value.

Some of the subfields of plant physiology are plant metabolism, or biochemistry; how water moves through plants; mineral nutrition required by plants for optimum growth; the growth and development of plants; plant response to environmental factors; and plant genetics.

In the past, plant physiologists have helped develop high crop yields. Work continues on plant pest control, reducing the effect of stresses such as drought and high soil salinity, improving crop yields, and applying the study of hormones and growth regulators to plant growth and development.

People who choose to be plant physiologists often do so because they have a strong love of plants, which they may have gained from growing up on a farm or being involved in other activities during youth. Plant physiologists perform varied work. The specialty a person chooses will determine the work setting, which may be a biochemistry laboratory, greenhouse, lecture hall, mountaintop or plateau, apple orchard, or wheat field. A definite reward of plant physiology is the opportunity to serve mankind through advancing knowledge or solving problems faced by those in agriculture, forestry, and range management.

Resource Management

All fifty states now have heritage programs. These are coordinated through The Nature Conservancy, and they employ field scientists to work in the field collecting data on ecosystems. Botanists work with these teams to inventory plants. Often these positions require advanced training.

Ecology

Salary Range: starting at about $19,500 with a bachelor's degree, $23,500 with a master's
Educational Requirements: college
Employment Outlook: excellent

Ecology is the study of the interactions among all types of life and, specifically, between an organism and its environment. Interaction is a key concept in the study of ecology. A variety of concentrations are possible within the field. For example, an ecologist may study specific organisms, such as microbes, plants, animals, or humans, or certain types of habitat, such as fresh or marine waters or land. Others may study different theories, work on experiments, or research specific problems or methods of understanding an ecological system. While some of this study may take place outdoors, much of it will be done in libraries, in laboratories, or at computer terminals.

Ecologists need a solid knowledge of the sciences. Although biology will be the base, other necessary courses include mathematics, basic statistics, and computer science. Spoken and written communications are vital to ecologists because financial support and action on problems may hinge on how effectively a problem or research need has been presented. Writing reports and analyses are also part of the job. Skill in communications, gained through coursework as well as practice, is a must.

The variety of jobs in the field of ecology is tremendous. The positions usually call for a specialization, such as aquatic ecology, wildlife ecology, or terrestrial ecology.

Ecologists find positions with consulting companies, industries, and the government. Other possibilities include teaching and research. Because of the increase in concern about our environment, jobs for ecologists have increased. Competition is very keen, however, and top achievers with the best background will have the edge in obtaining these jobs.

See Profile, page 55.

Veterinary Medicine

Salary Range: starting at about $23,800; average $48,600

Educational Requirements: advanced degree

Employment Outlook: good

Veterinarians today care for the health and well-being of animals and, indirectly, the people who own them. Their education and training is quite rigorous and is specifically aimed at the prevention, diagnosis, and treatment of animal health problems. Diagnosis will often involve tests, X rays, and the use of other equipment. Treatment may require setting a fracture, prescribing medication, delivering baby animals, and performing surgery.

Well over half of all veterinarians in the United States today work in private practice. They work on both ends of the health scale, preventing and treating disease and health problems. About half of these practitioners work with small animals, mostly pets such as cats and dogs. About 11 percent work with large animals— cattle, hogs, sheep, and horses. Many others have a mixed practice, which means they deal with both small and large animals.

The type of veterinary work that is most likely to involve working outdoors, often in inclement weather, is the large-animal practice. Veterinarians treating farm and ranch animals also spend a fair amount of time driving to patients that cannot be brought into their offices.

Veterinarians also may teach others to provide veterinary services. Closely allied with teaching is research, in which veterinarians seek to prevent and find solutions to animal health problems. This research has also contributed directly to solutions for many human health problems. Veterinarians are employed in private industry for research and development, private testing and animal research, or possibly marketing.

Two additional veterinary fields are regulatory medicine and public health. In regulatory medicine, veterinarians work to control or eradicate animal diseases and to protect the populace from those diseases that also affect humans. Public health work is done for various branches of government and involves controlling diseases and promoting health.

Some veterinarians work in the military service, where they may be involved in biomedical research and development or other research, food hygiene and safety, or treating government-owned animals. Others work in zoos and in aquatic animal medicine. A few work in space medicine and wildlife management. Other settings include animal shelters, racetracks, fur ranches, and circuses.

To obtain a veterinary degree, seven years of college education must be completed: three years of preveterinary education and four years in a school of veterinary medicine.

A major reward is the satisfaction of engaging in a respected profession that makes contributions to the health of society. The private practitioner also has the satisfaction of seeing sick animals recover and of assisting in keeping animals well. Self-employed private practitioners can set their own hours and work beyond normal retirement age. Their daily work may be quite varied and interesting. Veterinarians who work for the government, private firms, or colleges usually have pleasant working conditions, regular hours, and a steady income with good retirement programs and fringe benefits. Satisfaction from teaching and being involved in research programs are other rewards.

On the other hand, the hours for a new private practitioner can be long and irregular; the settings may be varied and possibly include dealing with bad weather. Bookwork, personnel, and other business matters are part of the details to work out in a private practice.

Some fields related to veterinary medicine are animal technology, animal husbandry, animal welfare, biological sciences, wildlife conservation, teaching, and research.

Veterinary technology is a related career. Veterinary technicians may assist veterinarians or work in laboratories, research, public health, or pharmaceutical manufacture. Educational programs vary somewhat; some involve two and others four years of study.

A veterinary technician will be trained on the job for the specific skills and procedures of a particular job. New graduates will know how to handle the usual species of animals treated and to perform routine laboratory procedures, and will be familiar with common drugs, instruments, and equipment.

See Profile, page 58.

Zoology

Salary Range: starting between $16,300 and $20,200 with a master's degree, $27,000 with a doctorate, up to $54,000 with experience

Educational Requirements: advanced degree

Employment Outlook: good, especially with a doctorate

Zoology, the study of animals, is another broad field in the biological sciences. Zoology has many subfields dealing with all aspects of animal life, from microscopic cells to the study of a specific animal or interaction among animals. A zoologist may study the biology of a specific group of animals; for example, a herpetologist studies snakes, a mammalogist studies mammals, and a carcinologist studies crabs. Other specific areas of study involve the structure of organisms (morphology), the function of organisms (physiology), and how an organism develops and passes its characteristics on to another generation (developmental science).

Persons who want a career in this field will begin by studying the broad area of animal biology and then go into a specialty when the area of most interest to them becomes clear. To allow for the most job opportunities in the field, it is wise to get a broad undergraduate background that includes courses in basic math, chemistry, and physics before concentrating too exclusively on an area of particular interest. To work in many fields, such as environmental science or marine biology, additional graduate training is required.

Academic institutions employ many animal biologists as either teachers or researchers or both. Teaching at the secondary level generally involves a broad knowledge of the field and includes teaching other science courses; a master's degree will add considerably to the knowledge and background required. College or university teaching requires specialization in one or more disciplines, and a doctorate is usually necessary.

Other possibilities for zoologists include museum work as a curator or setting up educational displays. Positions like this are limited in number and are quite competitive, as are positions for zoologists in zoos. Industry offers a variety of opportunities in areas such as pollution reduction or pest control using biological agents. Jobs in pharmaceutical or chemical firms include sales and the testing of compounds.

Many federal government agencies hire zoologists, including the Public Health Service, the Fish and Wildlife Service, the National Park Service, the Department of Agriculture, the Food and Drug Administration, the Smithsonian Institution, the National Academy of Sciences, and the National Oceanic and Atmospheric Administration. State conservation commissions and fish and game commissions are other government employers of zoologists. Additional employment may be found as a science librarian or science writer.

Working with Animals

Salary Range: caretakers can earn about $16,000 and up a year; trainers earn about $21,500 and up a year

Educational Requirements: on-the-job training, although biology courses are an asset

Employment Outlook: fair

A variety of careers involve working with animals. Zoos, aquariums, circuses, and amusement parks need animal caretakers for feeding, cleaning, and cage maintenance. Their general responsibility is to ensure that the animals are in good health for public view.

Circuses and amusement parks also employ animal trainers to work with the animals and train them to do certain stunts or tricks. Usually a trainer works with only one breed, such as lions, tigers, or elephants. Trainers are often involved in feeding, cleaning, and other maintenance tasks for the animals with which they work.

Another career that involves working with animals and some outdoor work is pet sitting. Pet sitters, who take care of animals whose owners are away from home, flourish in large urban centers. Their services may include outdoor exercise for dogs. Some urban areas have also seen the establishment of "doggie play groups," where a person with outdoor space will take care of a number of dogs in a manner somewhat like a day-care center for children.

Although no specialized training is required for working with animals, high school is a minimal requirement and biology courses are beneficial. Many aquariums, zoos, and circuses provide on-the-job training, but experience with animals can be a plus in obtaining these jobs. This experience can be gained through volunteer work at an animal shelter or by working for a veterinarian.

Zoos, aquariums, and amusement parks are becoming more popular, and some of the large zoos and parks are expanding. This means that there will continue to be positions that involve working with animals. In fact, as the move to provide better conditions for animals in these artificial environments continues, more jobs may open up for animal workers.

See Profile, page 60.

Resources
Agricultural Research Service
Information on working for the U.S. Department of Agriculture's Agricultural Research Service is available from U.S. Department of Agriculture, Agricultural Research Service, Personnel Division, Building 003, BARC-W, Beltsville, MD 20705.

Biological Sciences
Careers in Biology, II (pamphlet), American Institute of Biological Sciences, 730 11th Street, N.W., Washington, DC 20001-4584 (202-628-1500)

Botany
Careers in Botany (published by the Botanical Society of America), American Journal of Botany, 1735 Neil Avenue, Columbus, OH 43210.

Resource Management
Information about positions in the natural heritage program is available from The Nature Conservancy, Science Division, 1815 North Lynn Street, Arlington, VA 22209.

Ecology
Careers in Ecology, Ecological Society of America, Center for Environmental Studies, Arizona State University, Tempe, AZ 85287.

Plant Pathology
Careers in Plant Pathology, The American Phytopathological Society, 3340 Pilot Knob Road, St. Paul, MN 55121.

Plant Physiology
American Society of Plant Physiologists, P.O. Box 1688, Rockville, MD 20850.

Veterinary Medicine
Today's Veterinarian, Your Career in Veterinary Technology, and other pamphlets on veterinary medicine are available from American Veterinary Medical Association, 930 North Meacham Road, Schaumburg, IL 60196.

Zoology
Careers in Animal Biology, American Society of Zoologists, 104 Sirius Circle, Thousand Oaks, CA 91360.

Aquatic Biologist
Mark Hersh

Mark Hersh became an aquatic biologist because, he says, "I've always been interested in fishing and streams." Hersh's position with the Pennsylvania Department of Environmental Research is officially titled water pollution biologist, but he feels that aquatic biologist more accurately describes his work.

Hersh has a bachelor's degree in biology and an inter-disciplinary master's in water resources. This is essential background for the job, in which he uses water chemistry and biological data to assess the health of an aquatic system. To ascertain the physical characteristics of a stream, he takes samples of the water for chemical analysis and of the fish. Plants, including the microscopic algae, insect forms, and other invertebrates, are also studied.

"We collect data in summer and analyze it in winter, compiling it into a report," Hersh explains. "Sometimes we review reports done by private firms. I also spend time in meetings with, for example, persons seeking permits or representatives of the Environmental Protection Agency. We need to work with federal law and the programs delegated to the states."

Hersh says that any type of human activity relating to a body of water affects the biology of the water. He often investigates pollution spills or fish-kills. "Sometimes we study individual organisms and other times the whole system. Then we recommend the level of protection the stream should get. I must know what to expect in any system so I can find out if it is disturbed or not and what the human impact has been. Cause-and-effect relationships are elusive."

In addition to his specialized knowledge, Hersh needs to know taxonomy and must be able to use reference materials. Writing skills are also important for the numerous reports. Another essential skill for an aquatic biologist is the ability to work with people. On his job, Hersh deals with other professionals, the public, and information specialists.

The mix of indoor-outdoor work for aquatic biologists depends on the position and the season. "In the summer I spend 60 to 80 percent of my time outside in good weather," Hersh says. "Some will spend a majority of their time outdoors, and others none at all. As you advance up the career ladder, you get less outdoor work.

"We call ourselves 'windshield surveyors' because our responsibility encompasses the whole state. We may spend more time getting to the location than we spend in the stream," he comments wryly.

Patience with the bureaucracy is a desirable personality trait for Hersh's position. "It is also important to derive satisfaction from doing your job and doing it well," he acknowledges realistically, "because the monetary rewards are not that great."

What is Hersh's advice for someone who is interested in becoming an aquatic biologist? "Question your motives. Ask yourself why you want to do this. Don't do this if you think it consists of walking through woods looking at pretty streams. Before you get into this career, make sure it is what you want to do.

"If you want to be an environmental activist, there are other ways to accomplish the same ends. This is a field where citizen activists can make a difference. Activism pays more and allows you to live anywhere. Volunteering may allow you to have the same or greater impact. Trout Unlimited is one group with knowledgeable lay people."

Hersh mentions that some negatives of his job include limited opportunities and potential for advancement. Also, he says, "The job you want might not be in a great geographic location."

But his job does have its advantages. "With government work there is no client to please. And I like streams as a system. It is a big puzzle to try to work out."

See Aquatic Biology, page 40.

Ecologist
Rebecca Sharitz

"Ecologists need to have a strong curiosity about the functioning of natural systems," Rebecca Sharitz declares. "In some areas of ecology, it also helps to be enthusiastic about outdoor activities and not mind being occasionally muddy, dirty, uncomfortable, and wet."

Sharitz should know. She is a professor of ecology in the department of botany at the University of Georgia and spends a major part of her time at the University's Savannah River Ecology Laboratory (SREL). There she is senior research ecologist and the head of the Division of Wetlands Ecology, directing a $2.8 million program that employs seven Ph.D.s and several postdoctoral fellows. She also supervises the research activities of a number of graduate students.

Her decision to enter the field of ecology was strongly influenced by her youth on a rural Virginia farm, her desire to do research in an outdoor environment, and the contagious enthusiasm of the professor of her first college ecology course. She has a bachelor's degree in biology and a doctorate in botany with a major in ecology.

Sharitz conducts research to determine the effects of human activities on forest wetland habitats, such as those along the major rivers in the southeastern United States. "By changing the flood patterns of rivers through construction of dams and reservoirs we impact adjacent swamps and floodplain forests," Sharitz explains. "I study the effects of these man-made changes on the population biology of wetland plants." She has been working at several research sites along the Savannah River for nearly twenty years. "To evaluate the effects of human activities on the environment, we must understand natural ecological processes. So, much of my research is also on undisturbed populations of wetland plants."

Since Hurricane Hugo slashed through the eastern United States in 1989, Sharitz has also conducted research in the Congaree Swamp National Monument in South Carolina, a wilderness area of the national park system. Here she studies the degree of disturbance and the timing of recovery from the effects of Hugo on the bottomland hardwood forests. This study of the effects of a natural event—the hurricane—complements her research on human impact on the environment.

Sharitz says there is no such thing as a typical day or week on her job. One recent week found her spending two days at the University of Georgia, although she normally visits the campus only once a week, devoting the greatest amount of her time to research at the SREL. On Monday she attended the final seminar of one of her Ph.D. students. On Tuesday she taught a course. Wednesday was spent in her research office at SREL, writing a scientific paper, reviewing manuscripts, and meeting with students and other researchers. Thursday she was in the Congaree Swamp from dawn until dusk, mapping and measuring trees to check their recovery from the hurricane. On Friday she analyzed data and tended to various types of administrative paperwork.

Ideal preparation for a career in ecology, according to Sharitz, should include a broad background in biology and chemistry in addition to ecology. "Don't narrow your focus too early in your academic studies, but build a broad base of knowledge," she emphasizes. "For my field a good understanding of natural history—plants, animals, soils, and geology—is important." Solid training in statistics and in mathematics, as well as a facility with a variety of computer programs, can be extremely valuable.

"Writing is another critical skill," she adds. "You must be able to communicate the results of your research effectively. Speaking skills are also important for expressing ideas at scientific meetings and for teaching." Depending on the specific research interests of an ecologist, certain foreign language skills can be an asset. Foreign languages may be necessary for conducting research in other countries.

According to Sharitz, the greatest number of ecology positions today appear to be in environmental consulting, with industries, or with state and local governments. For these positions, a master's degree is becoming a necessity. Academic positions in ecology, which require a doctorate, seem to be dwindling.

Aspects of her job that Sharitz enjoys most are working outdoors and working with other outdoor people, although she admits ruefully that she used to spend more time out in the field than she can now. Her job now requires that she spend a lot of time preparing reports and doing paperwork involved with quality control and compliance with governmental regulations. "These activities may be important, but they do take the scientist's time away from the actual science," she says.

See Ecology, page 46.

Veterinarian
Donna Matthews

"As a kid I always wanted to be a vet, and I started working with a vet after school when I was 16," says Donna Matthews, a veterinarian in Luray, Virginia. Nevertheless, she found it difficult to translate her childhood dream into reality. As a college freshman she applied to veterinary school but was refused admission—in the early 1970s veterinary schools accepted few women. This pattern persisted throughout her four years of college, and after graduating with a bachelor's degree in animal science, she worked at a sheep farm run by the National Institutes of Health. Ten years after her first application, Matthews finally gained admission to veterinary school. She says that now veterinary school classes are about half male and half female.

Matthews specializes in small ruminants—sheep and llamas—although her practice includes other animals. Llamas, says Matthews, are good farm animals for the farmer who doesn't want to invest a lot of money and equipment in farming; quite a lot of them are raised in her area. "Llamas have a lot of personality, their babies are incredible, and the people that raise them are very interesting," she says enthusiastically. "Because we in North America don't know a lot about llamas, we are breaking new ground as we deal with them. It's quite a challenge."

Matthews spends from half to three-quarters of her time outside. She begins a typical day in her clinic, examining hospitalized patients and taking in-clinic appointments. By late morning she is outdoors, where she stays until late afternoon when she returns to the clinic. She says, however, that her schedule is not at all typical of other outdoor veterinarians: "There are many different outside vets and each one does it differently."

In her outdoor visits she checks to see how many animals are pregnant and if the males are fertile. She also keeps her outdoor patients on a careful health regimen that includes regular vaccinations.

"My job is very challenging and at times very rewarding. On pretty days there is nothing better than playing outside with sheep on a farm." Matthews says that scheduling her visits to Luray-area farms can be a real challenge.

She admits candidly that there are many things she doesn't like about her career. "The lifestyle is terrible. I am on call continually—my clients don't accept other vets but want me to attend to problems. I also have to be all things to all people at all times—I have to work with every system on every creature even though I am more comfortable in my specialty." She concedes, however, that this is probably more typical of a rural veterinary practice than an urban one.

She adds: "To stay with this career you must really want to do it. The pay is not equal to almost any other career for which you spend this amount of time in preparation. Because the thing I enjoy most about my work is the medicine, I often think I should have gone to medical school." Had she done so, she believes her compensation would be more in line with the time she spent training for her career.

Contrary to many expectations, veterinary work is very people-intensive, Matthew notes. "People sometimes say to me, 'I want to be a vet because I just want to work with animals.' This is a misconception. I spend a great deal of my time dealing with people, not just working with animals."

Matthews suggests that a broad background in undergraduate studies, not just a focus on science, is the best preparation for veterinary school, which takes four years.

Her advice to would-be vets: "Make sure you really want to get into this career. Spend time with a practitioner seeing how much work it is and how much of a total commitment it really is."

See Veterinary Medicine, page 47.

Elephant Trainer
April Yoder

"Lady, leave it!" Elephant trainer April Yoder speaks firmly and carries a small stick. Beside the elephants, the five-foot-six Yoder looks diminutive. "When you give a command, you have to sound authoritative," she says. "You can say it very softly as long as you say it with authority."

Her enthusiasm for her job is obvious. "I love working with the elephants. Each one has a different personality, and I like to be able to get close to them and develop a relationship with them. They're very challenging animals. They have such excellent memories and are so intelligent."

Yoder's route to her present job was just a few short steps from her graduation with a bachelor of science in biology. She says that, although she has always loved animals, she didn't major in zoology because she thought it was too specific. She felt that a biology major would give her more opportunities and enable her to go in many directions.

"I always knew I would work with animals," Yoder relates. "I didn't want to work in a lab or inside because I'm an outdoors-type person. Despite my degree, I wasn't sure where I would be able to find a job, because I had zero experience. So when I found a ten-month seasonal position here, I was ecstatic—it was everything I had ever dreamed of!"

Yoder has been with the elephants at Kings Dominion Park near Richmond, Virginia, for two years now. She says that seasonal employment is a good way to start. Or better yet, she suggests, become a seasonal volunteer so that you will have a chance to closely observe the elephants. Elephants sometimes do not like certain people, and seasonal work can give you a feel for whether this is what you want to do.

Asked what advice she'd give someone who wants to be an elephant trainer, Yoder responds without hesitation, "I'd tell them to go for it!" She then adds thoughtfully, "I'd tell them to think about it, because it's not something you can do for two months and then say, 'That's it.' The animals get used to you. You really have to make sure it's what you want to do."

About developing the important relationship between elephant and trainer, Yoder explains, "You get used to them at the same time they're getting used to you. When I first started working with elephants, I was absolutely petrified. I didn't really realize their size until I was right up on them.

"In this job you have to be very dedicated because the elephants require so much work. You have to put yourself wholeheartedly into it. And you have to pump yourself up when you walk into the barn to impress on them that you're in charge. It's called 'the elephant attitude.'"

Kings Dominion has two senior elephant handlers, with a third in training. For her first five months, Yoder worked as a junior, giving basic commands to the elephants. Her lucky break came with a staff turnover. After a month of intensive coaching (eight hours a day, five or six days a week) by noted movie-animal trainer Dave McMillan, she became a senior handler.

Her daily routine begins with a morning check to be sure the elephants are okay. At night they are loose in the barn, but now they are placed in chains for their morning feeding. In the summer they spend their days on Elephant Island, and in cooler weather they stay indoors.

"In the evening we bring them in and feed them, again in chains, then put them in the barn and let them loose. That's their day. Of course, we have to clean up—that's the best part," Yoder jokes. Other duties include "maintaining the exhibits, cutting the grass, fixing whatever breaks, carpentry work, and landscaping work. Most people here are jacks-of-all-trades."

In the spring, summer, and fall, Yoder spends four or five hours outdoors with the elephants, which she says is not enough. "During the wintertime we spend more time with them because they are here in the barn."

Yoder admits that one drawback of working with elephants is their unpredictability. "These guys are very docile. But elephants are the number one reason for deaths in zoos because of their size. They are so dangerous and unpredictable. Sometimes it's accidental, but not always. So when you're in the barn, you always have to be aware of where they are and what they're doing. That's why I carry the ankus stick around—for safety reasons." That is also why only designated elephant handlers are allowed to work with the elephants. Seasonals normally take care of the giraffes and white rhinos but have limited contact with the elephants, although they help take care of the elephant barn. "We have very strict rules because of the danger."

The only real down side of her job, Yoder confides, is that taking care of elephants can be very frustrating. "Yesterday was a perfect example. I got so frustrated because they wouldn't eat, and I worried about them. It's like a mother when her children are sick. Sometimes they can be like two-year-old children: You can do everything and they won't listen to you. And it's very hard to keep calm. It's a discipline you have to acquire."

How does one prepare to become an elephant handler? "All of the elephant work I do I basically learned hands-on," answers Yoder. "But my biology degree does help, because when I talk with the vet about medical problems, I can understand what she's saying. I'm more aware of what's going on because of having been taught about the scientific method and how to do research."

Yoder expects to stay with the elephants for a while longer. "Two years is not a lot of experience in some people's eyes; a lot of handlers have tended two years." Gaining additional experience will serve her well, she believes. Though not yet certain about her career path, Yoder sees the possibility of having her own facility. Management has less appeal because it would mean spending little time with the elephants themselves.

See Working with Animals, page 50.

"In wildness is the preservation of the world."
Henry David Thoreau

Conservation

Conservation is generally defined as the management, preservation, and careful use of natural resources—air, water, soil, minerals, plants, and animals—for economic or recreational purposes. The need for conservation in the United States did not became apparent to many until the late nineteenth century. At that time the move to conserve natural resources was largely a response to the flagrant killing of North American wildlife such as the beaver and the buffalo.

The ideas of conservation had been promoted by prominent American naturalists such as John James Audubon, Henry David Thoreau, George Perkins Marsh, and John Muir as early as the 1850s. The first national park in the world—Yellowstone National Park—was established in 1872.

Conservation gained status as a national movement in the early 1900s. Under the presidency of Theodore Roosevelt, the first federal wildlife refuge—Pelican Island, Florida—was established, and more than 140 million acres were added to the national forest reserves.

An impetus to this emerging movement came when a major White House conference, attended by governors, federal officials, scientists, business executives, and conservationists, was held in 1908. Convened to set national conservation policies, one result of this conference was the decision to use public lands for purposes other than commercial development. Another far-reaching outcome was the establishment soon afterward of conservation commissions in forty-one states.

The term *conservation* was apparently first used by Gifford Pinchot, who headed the U.S. Forest Service during Theodore

Roosevelt's administration. Early efforts at conservation centered on preserving forests and wildlife. The need for soil conservation was dramatized in the early 1930s when the disaster generally known as the Dust Bowl hit the Great Plains. During this time, windstorms blew away the fertile topsoil, which had been damaged by poor farming and ranching practices and a prolonged drought. Because of this disastrous experience the term *conservation* now encompasses soil science in addition to forestry and wildlife biology.

Careers related to conservation are many and varied. They generally involve management of and education about resources. Landscaping careers increasingly relate to conservation, and they are also covered in this chapter.

Park Management

Salary Range: varies with employer; between $16,500 and $38,000 for park rangers with U.S. Park Service. Interpreters make between $19,000 and $29,000

Educational Requirements: some park ranger positions require only a two-year associate's degree; for other positions, including interpretation, a bachelor's degree is minimum

Employment Outlook: retirements will open up park ranger positions but these will be very competitive; interpreter positions are more recent and are tied to the economy—in tight financial situations they are among the first to be cut

Park management work in the western national parks was originally performed by U.S. Army troops. Civilian park rangers replaced the troops when the National Park Service was formed in 1916. The image of the park ranger has changed in recent years; it no longer is that of a person whose noble and generous character has been shaped by long periods in the remote outdoor reaches of a large wilderness park. With the creation of more urban parks, and following the 1970 riots in Yosemite Park, more emphasis has had to be placed on law enforcement. Additionally, the ecological impacts of all actions are now of more concern to rangers.

The majority of park ranger positions are with the federal government through the National Park Service, a bureau of the U.S. Department of the Interior. State and county parks also provide job possibilities for park rangers, although they may not be as large or as well staffed as their federal counterparts. Additionally, there are many privately owned and operated parks, such as the historical parks at Colonial Williamsburg, Old Sturbridge Village, and Monticello, the home of Thomas Jefferson.

The U.S. Park Service

The National Park Service oversees the National Park System. Four basic types of parks exist: natural, cultural, historical, and recreational. Some parks, of course, have more than one of these functions. There are about 321 units and some 77 million acres of national park land in forty-nine states (all but Delaware); plus Puerto Rico, Guam, and the Virgin Islands. The two main goals of the Park Service are to save the natural and cultural resources of the country and to give the public access to recreational, inspirational, and educational experiences.

More than half of all park rangers in the United States work in areas east of the Mississippi River. While much of their work is conducted in the outdoors, office work is also necessary. As rangers advance into managerial positions, they spend more and more time indoors in meetings, writing reports, and performing other managerial tasks.

Four types of jobs are held by park rangers: historical interpretation, natural interpretation, resource management, and law enforcement. The exact tasks of each ranger position will depend on the type of job and the park. Not all parks have all of these positions. For example, the National Capital Region has few full-time law enforcement positions because the park police provide this service. Parks in other regions do have law enforcement positions. The type of park also influences the variety of positions available. Some parks, such as Yosemite, Yellowstone, and Mesa Verde, are like small cities, and park ranger positions include functions such as sewer maintenance and fire management.

Competition for park ranger positions is very keen, and these jobs are difficult to obtain. Tests are given for jobs, and since they are usually given on very short notice, the accident of timing—being available when the tests are given—may be crucial. Another strategy is to stay aware of jobs available at the park or parks in which you are interested by calling the national park region job line.

Park Resource Management

A park ranger in charge of resource management has an incredible variety of tasks. These often involve interaction with persons living or owning land near the park. For example, one responsibility of a resource manager is the control of gypsy moths and other infestations. Rangers patrol the park area looking for evidence of gypsy moths, such as egg masses on trees. If evidence is found and the area needs to be sprayed, adjacent landowners must be notified in advance of the spraying. Duties also include keeping walking trails in good shape for hikers and dealing with other issues relating to park resources as they arise.

In addition to a knowledge of natural resources, a park ranger in charge of resource management needs people skills, as there is constant interaction with users of the park and contact with adjacent landowners. Excellent verbal communication skills are essential, as are writing skills for handling reports and other necessary writing.

See Profile, page 80.

Interpretation

Interpreters, or naturalists, are responsible for communicating information about nature and the environment and how these relate to people. This can be done through talks, tours, museum displays, or newsletters. Some interpreters are classified as park rangers in national or other large parks.

Interpreters come from several academic backgrounds: natural resources, such as biology, forestry, or soils; education; and history. Communications courses are important background for writing press releases, reports, and brochures, and for working with the electronic media. Computer literacy and administrative skills are also important.

Although the work settings and employers are quite varied, most employers are parks and recreation areas, museums, educational settings, and organizations concerned with different aspects of the environment. The educational background required for interpretation jobs varies according to the position, but a bachelor's degree is usually necessary and advanced degrees may be required for some levels of work. Parks and recreation areas have many seasonal (usually summer) interpretation jobs. Seasonal or internship positions are typical first jobs for naturalist interpreters. In fact, many work in these types of positions for years.

Interpretive naturalist positions, especially with the government, are strongly influenced by the economic climate. Because the field is new, these jobs are often the first to be dropped with belt-tightening.

See Profile, page 82.

Fish and Wildlife Management

Salary Range: starting between $14,500 and $19,500; average $26,000 with experience
Educational Requirements: master's degree for the best opportunities
Employment Outlook: jobs expected to increase at a slow rate

The fish and wildlife manager is one of a number of professional resource managers, which also include forest rangers, park naturalists, and range managers. The term *wildlife* applies to animals that are not domesticated. The fish and wildlife manager is often interested in game animals that are harvested for food or sport. Nongame species such as songbirds and small animals are also a concern. Fish are technically a type of wildlife that is often placed in a separate category; fish and their habitat are also managed by the fish and wildlife manager.

The fish and wildlife manager needs to ensure that populations of wildlife are maintained at satisfactory levels. The job entails gathering data through research and applying scientific solutions to problems facing a particular species, and it may involve habitat maintenance. Enforcement of regulations controlling hunting and fishing seasons are also among the responsibilities.

A very important part of the work of the fish and wildlife manager is education. Informing others about the management and ecology of wildlife through work at a nature or conservation center is important for the future of wildlife.

Background for fish and wildlife management should include general science courses, such as botany, zoology, ecology, hydrology, and geology, plus social sciences and communications. It is recommended that one or more courses be taken at a field or biological station.

A bachelor's degree in wildlife management or fisheries science may lead to only part-time or temporary jobs in the field. A master's degree is now becoming essential for a career in this field; most of the jobs advertised call for one. A master's degree usually leads to a job managing resources or to an administrative position. A doctorate is essential for university teaching, research positions, or consulting work.

The government is the major employer of fish and wildlife managers, especially the state conservation agencies, as well as federal government departments such as the Fish and Wildlife Service. Some city and county governments in high-population areas also need such specialists. Jobs with private industries and management positions also exist. Positions in teaching and research are available for those with graduate level training.

See Profile, page 84.

Forest Management

Salary Range: foresters with the federal government start at about $17,500, average $26,000 to $28,000; private employment is similar with doctorate holders earning $27,000 plus. Forest technicians generally earn between $16,000 and $20,000

Educational Requirements: foresters need minimum

of bachelor's degree, a master's for research, and a master's or doctorate for teaching; forest technicians need high school plus on-the-job training or two-year technician's degree

Employment Outlook: slow increase in jobs for foresters and forest technicians; they will be very competitive, however, with many qualified for forester jobs taking technician jobs

Forestry work involves managing and using the forests and related natural resources to benefit humans. This requires knowledge about soil, air, water, trees and other plants, wild and domestic animals, and the interrelationship of all these factors.

Work with people and issues related to use of the land by the public is also part of forest management. Skills in relating to people and problem solving are essential in this career. Two of the more common positions in forest management are forester and forest technician.

The U.S. Forest Service

The U.S. Forest Service, a part of the Department of Agriculture, is probably the single largest employer of foresters and forest technicians in the country. There are more positions for forestry technicians than for foresters with the government. Some persons with qualifications for forester positions take technician positions; a limited number of these later move into positions as foresters.

A typical career path with the Forest Service would start with work as a seasonal employee before obtaining a permanent job. Administrative positions in the Forest Service are, in ascending order, district ranger, forester, forest supervisor, and chief of forest service.

Persons interested in becoming a district ranger must compete for the job. If someone does not want to go into administrative work as a district ranger, there are other options at the same grade level. These are specialty positions, such as work with timber, recreation, wildlife, or engineering. Higher grades include positions as supervisors in regional offices or in the Washington office. Professionals in the Forest Service have opportunities to move around. There is, in fact, a mobility policy: Persons move to get promotions.

In July 1990 the Forest Service began to experiment with a different method of hiring. Previously, persons interested in forestry positions were hired from a central listing. Almost two-thirds of the new employees had worked with the Forest Service as co-op students, so the number taken from this list was fairly low. In this new experiment, which will run until July 1995, three-fourths of the jobs will be advertised and hired locally, not from this central listing. This will probably mean that fewer co-op students will be hired and local candidates may have a better chance of getting available jobs. Jobs for foresters will remain very competitive, however. Technician jobs have always been advertised locally.

The Forest Service is experiencing a steady number of retirements in forestry positions and will continue to do so until 2002. Although this should open up some job opportunities, the number of these positions may be in decline because of such issues as the cutting of old-growth forests and economic problems. The greatest amount of hiring in the Forest Service is currently for wildlife biologists, fishery biologists, and law enforcement personnel. The Forest Service is trying to increase the variety of ways that national forests are used.

Forestry

Some of the duties a forester performs include planting, measuring, and grading trees; supervising timber harvesting; developing plans for recreation areas; managing, in cooperation with states, wildlife habitats (for big game, small game, and fish) and planning to ensure an abundance of wildlife; managing watersheds for flood control, timber production, and soil conservation; evaluating and managing insect and disease outbreaks; and planning roads and trails.

A college degree, with strong emphasis on science and math, is important for forestry work. Forestry curricula at the many accredited forestry schools in the United States concentrate on the biological, physical, and social sciences and also now have more emphasis on sociology and psychology. The ability to work with others in group interaction, problem solving, and marketing is essential, especially for people in management positions. Writing and public speaking courses are also important background for forester positions.

Entry-level forestry jobs are very competitive, and graduates with top marks will have an advantage in job hunting. Summer work experience in a forestry job will also be a plus. It is government policy that the various agency work forces should have percentages of minorities and women similar to those in the civilian labor force. Although the number of women in forestry has increased in recent years, both the government and private organizations are recruiting more minorities for forestry positions.

Often foresters advance from hands-on, outdoor-work, entry-level positions to administrative positions that are largely performed indoors. Administrators oversee organizational work, planning, budget preparation and management, report preparation, and contracting.

One reason forestry positions are attractive is the opportunity to be immersed in the natural environment. Although many foresters live and work in rural settings, numerous positions for foresters are also available in or near large urban areas.

Foresters find jobs in municipal, county, state, and federal settings. Other positions are available in universities and schools, with industrial associations, and for citizens' organizations. Forest products companies are one type of industry that needs foresters. Management positions exist in conservation organizations, public agencies involved in land management, and private industries. Some persons also work as private consulting foresters.

See Profile, page 86.

Forest Technology

Work performed by forest technicians is markedly similar to that of the forester, but technicians usually work under the supervision of foresters to accomplish daily jobs, while foresters work in management and planning, and apply their training to the task at hand. The pay and possibilities for career advancement are not as good for technicians as for foresters.

Technicians work mainly in the outdoors. Some of the tasks they perform include measuring and recording tree height and diameter, thinning young stands of timber to improve productivity, recording rain gauge data, maintaining public camping areas, and working as fire fighters or on fire lookout duty.

Forest technicians must have completed a two-year forest technology course or had on-the-job training. Having the technician's degree will be a help in job advancement.

Conservation District Work

Salary Range: administrative positions from $48,000 to $57,000; technical (depending on education and job requirements), $28,000 to $42,000; clerical, $22,000 to $28,000; public information, $25,000 to $32,000

Educational Requirements: depend on complexity of job; some positions require master's degree and doctorate

Employment Outlook: poor because of financial crunch facing states and counties, not lack of need

Under the U.S. Department of Agriculture, the country is organized into 2,926 conservation districts. These districts were established in 1937 in response to the great Dust Bowl disaster. They originally focused on soil conservation, but in most states their mandate has now broadened to include protection of all earth-based resources: soil, water, and wetlands.

A key function of these districts is planning, both annual and long-range. These plans become a program that identifies opportunities to develop and conserve local natural resources. The districts may also be charged with following through on state legislation, such as the Chesapeake Bay Preservation Act passed by the state of Virginia. This Act requires conservation plans to protect the Chesapeake Bay, and the appropriate districts review these plans to see if they will fulfill this function.

Conservation districts are found in all states; often one office will be in charge of several counties, with only one staff member or a part-time clerical person employed. In urban areas that have more problems, the offices will be larger. For example, the office that covers Fairfax County, Virginia—Northern Virginia Soil and Water Conservation District—employs seven full-time staffers.

This office has a number of positions that involve extensive outdoor work and training in fields such as conservation engineering, earth science, agronomy, and soil science.

Many of these districts do not have a separate telephone number but are listed under the Soil Conservation Service of the U.S. Department of Agriculture. Unfortunately, salaries in these offices are not usually competitive with jobs in industry. They do, however, offer jobs working to conserve the environment, good experience, and second careers for retired civil servants.

The district movement is founded on grass roots voluntarism, and many opportunities exist for volunteers to get involved. Volunteers may be high school or college students, retirees, or any other persons who want to spend some of their free time working for the environment. Volunteering with these districts is a good way to learn about them and about environmentally oriented work. To obtain district addresses, contact the National Association of Conservation Districts, listed under Resources at the end of this chapter.

Nursery and Landscaping

Salary Range: arborists' salaries range between $22,500 and $38,000 depending on skills needed and responsibilities of position; landscape architects start at about $20,000, average $36,000, and executives make about $76,000

Educational Requirements: some arborist positions require on-the-job training, others college; landscape architects need a four- to five-year bachelor's degree

Employment Outlook: generally good for arborists; landscape architect positions are cut back in a poor economy

The goal of the nursery and landscaping industry is to improve and protect the gifts of nature to provide a better environment for humans. The landscaping industry includes nursery operations such as wholesale growers, nursery and garden centers, and mail-order nurseries. Wholesale growers raise plants to sell to retail nurseries or landscaping firms. Nursery and garden centers are retail firms that sell plants and materials for gardening and lawn care, along with related products. And mail-order nurseries grow plants, then advertise and sell them through the mail.

Work in the industry varies from less technical jobs involving production and selling to more technical jobs that require knowledge of plants and diseases. Some agronomists, entomologists, and plant pathologists find work in this industry. Other typical positions include production managers and supervisors of skilled work such as cutting, germination of seeds, day-to-day growing of plants, transplanting, pruning, and staking. Persons knowledgeable about plants assemble orders, and others prepare and protect plants for shipping. Still others operate machinery such as forklifts and soil shredders. Quality-control positions also exist.

Persons interested in this type of work can take advantage of a variety of educational opportunities, including vocational courses in secondary school and two-year programs following high school. These often include some training in the field or related work experience. There are also four-year programs leading to a bachelor's degree, as well as advanced study. It is possible, too, to learn on the job and work upward through the ranks as knowledge and skills grow.

Arboriculture

An arborist takes care of trees and shrubs in the urban environment. The work includes selecting and planting the proper types of trees for a particular space, pruning, fertilizing, and pest control.

An arborist works mainly in the outdoors and must have good health and physical stamina, as well as the ability to work as part of a team. The work often involves using heavy equipment or equipment that demands manual dexterity and coordination, although the basic work of the arborist is done by hand. Some of the work will be done above the ground; this requires good balance.

A knowledge of trees and their care is a must in this career. This can be acquired through on-the-job training or college study. Work can be found in commercial firms that service trees and with parks, cities, and utility companies. It is an expanding field with opportunities at all levels of employment.

Landscape Architecture

Landscape architects deal with the relation of people to the environment. Designing public areas—parks, campuses, shopping centers, and industrial parks—so that they are beautiful as well as functional is the major task of landscape architects. In doing this, the landscape architect often works as part of a team with architects, engineers, planners, and horticulturists.

Traditionally, landscape architects designed parks and gardens; today that is just one specialty of the profession. Other specialties include landscape designing for hotels and resorts, shopping centers, and public or private housing. Some landscape architects prepare studies on cost, environmental impact, and feasibility or are involved in regional planning and resource management. Some not only design but supervise site work as well.

Working time is usually balanced between indoors and out: Part of the time is spent in the office preparing drawings and models and discussing these and cost estimates with clients, and part is spent outdoors studying and planning the sites and supervising the projects. Necessary personal qualities of landscape architects include an appreciation of nature, creativity, and artistic talent.

The minimum educational requirement is a bachelor's degree in landscaping design. High school courses that provide important background include mechanical or geometrical drawing, art, botany, and mathematics. Facility in written and spoken English is important for making group presentations and writing project proposals. Technical courses in college include surveying, graphics, structural design, and design and construction of landscapes. Also required are courses in horticulture and botany, planning, science, mathematics, English, and the social sciences.

This is a field of promise; however, its growth is tied to construction growth, which is determined by the economy. When construction is down, the demand for landscape architects is also reduced. During the 1980s, a boom period, work for landscape architects was plentiful. With the recession of the early 1990s, the situation has changed and the outlook for the near future is not yet clear.

See Profile, page 89.

Seasonal and Volunteer Work

The conservation field is one area that offers a wide variety of seasonal and volunteer employment. These positions, in addition to experience and knowledge of the field, may also lead to full-time positions.

The National Park System

Many people use seasonal work as a means to get into full-time employment with the National Park System. To do this successfully, it is advantageous to work in several different parks to get a wide range of experience.

When seasonal work peaks during the summer months, approximately 14,000 summer, part-time, and temporary employees work in national parks. Unfortunately, getting seasonal jobs is extremely difficult. These jobs are very competitive, especially those in the larger parks, and the number of applicants is far greater than the number of positions available. Obtaining seasonal positions in the smaller parks or for winter jobs is easier. Applicants with previous seasonal park experience, special skills needed for specific settings, or law enforcement experience or training will have an edge.

Volunteering time with the National Park Service is another way to gain experience, although volunteer work does not necessarily help one obtain paid employment in park positions. But certainly the relevant experience gained may give an edge in getting either a seasonal or a full-time position, and one can make good contacts as well. At the least, it may provide a satisfying sideline for persons otherwise employed.

Seasonal Fire Fighting

Each summer the Forest Service hires a number of seasonal employees to assist with fighting forest fires, mostly in the western states of Alaska, California, Montana, Oregon, and Utah. For these fire fighters, or smoke jumpers, the work is heavy and extensive training is necessary. New smoke jumpers usually receive about four weeks of training, and experienced jumpers generally get a week of refresher training. These positions require some previous fire-fighting experience and a season of general forest experience. Many people apply for these positions, but few are selected because previous fire-fighting experience, rigid physical conditioning, and excellent health are all required.

Since summer workers are usually selected in December of the previous year, interested persons should apply early. Application can be made through the Forest Service or at state employment offices. The application form is the standard U.S. government SF171 form.

Resources

Arboriculture
Municipal Arborists and Urban Foresters Society, P.O. Box 1255, Freehold, NJ 07728-1255.

Conservation District Work
For local addresses, contact National Association of Conservation Districts, P.O. Box 855, League City, TX 77574-0855 (713-332-3402).

Fish and Wildlife Management
Planning a Career in Fish and Wildlife Management (pamphlet), International Association of Fish and Wildlife Agencies, 444 North Capitol Street, N.W., Suite 534, Washington, DC 20001 (202-624-7890).

Forestry
Career Profiles; Careers: Professional and Administrative Careers in the Forest Service; Forestry Schools in the United States; Forests & Forestry in the U.S.A.; A Job with the Forest Service; A Job with the Forest Service: A Guide to Career Opportunities in Technical Support Positions; and *What the Forest Service Does* (pamphlets), U.S. Department of Agriculture, Forestry Service, P.O. Box 96090, Washington, DC 20013-6090.
Forests & Forestry in the U.S.A., a booklet containing overall information on forests but not specific career information, is

available for $1.50 from American Forestry Association, P.O. Box 2000, Washington, DC 20013.

So You Want to Be in Forestry ($.40), *Career Information Question and Answer Sheet, Job Seekers' Guide,* and sheet listing accredited professional forestry degree programs and recognized technical forestry education programs are available from Society of American Foresters, 5400 Grosvenor Lane, Bethesda, MD 20814, (301-897-8720).

Seasonal Fire Fighting
U.S. Forestry Service, Federal Center, Bldg. 85, Denver, CO 80255.

The National Park System
Anzalone, Dave, ed. *National Parks Trade Journal,* 3d ed. Yosemite National Park, CA: Taverly Churchill Publishing, 1989. This book includes helpful articles on working in the National Park System and useful information about the different parks, international work, and ski resorts. The 352-page third edition is available for $15.50 from Dave Anzalone, Taverly Churchill Publishing, Wawona Station, Yosemite National Park, CA 95389 (209-375-6552).

National Park Service: Careers, a booklet giving general information on both the National Park Service and available careers, and *Seasonal Employment: The National Parks,* a brochure giving overall information on seasonal jobs, are available from U.S. Department of the Interior, National Park Service, P.O. Box 37127, Washington, DC 20013-7127.

V.I.P., Volunteers in Parks and *National Park Service Volunteers,* brochures on volunteer opportunities, are available from regional Park Service offices. Obtain these phone numbers or addresses from your local library or the booklet *National Park Service: Careers* listed above.

The following are National Park System job line numbers with listings of park positions.

North Atlantic Region: 617-223-5111
Mid-Atlantic Region: 215-597-4971
National Capital Region: 202-619-7111

Southeast Region: 404-331-5714
Midwest Region: 402-221-3456
Southwest Region: 505-988-6641
Western Region: 415-556-4196
Rocky Mountain Region: 303-969-2770
Pacific Northwest Region: 206-442-4409
Alaska: 907-257-2574

Park Ranger Resource Manager
Hank Snyder

"I always liked the outdoors and thought working in parks would be a good job," responds Hank Snyder to the question of why he chose this career. Over the years, he has worked in two state parks in California, for the U.S. Bureau of Land Management, and in six different national parks. He is currently a national park ranger at the George Washington Memorial Parkway in the Virginia suburbs of Washington, D.C. The George Washington Memorial Parkway, developed as a memorial to George Washington, maintains the natural scenery of the Potomac River in this highly urban setting and leads to Washington's home, Mount Vernon, south of the Capitol.

Snyder began his park career in a maintenance job picking up trash on a beach and moved up in successive positions to his current post as a ranger resource manager. This progression through the ranks is fairly typical for park rangers.

"I spend 50 percent of my time outdoors and 50 percent indoors," explains Snyder. "Most people in these positions wish that they were outdoors more, but I like this mix. I have, however, turned down desk jobs." He admits that the pay is not high and adds wryly, "Park rangers have the saying that we 'get paid in sunsets.'"

Snyder has a bachelor's degree in geology and a master's in earth sciences. Although he doesn't use the coursework in his position, he certainly uses the skills that helped him get the degrees: writing, communications, and research. "The case reports, interpretive programs, and letters require good writing skills. Speaking is essential, because we are almost an entertainment industry. We must be able to relate to people."

Snyder lists helpful personality attributes for park rangers as being gregarious, tolerant, and flexible. "We must be gregarious because we are constantly relating to people and tolerant because we deal with many people who may ask very obvious questions. Flexibility is important because we deal with so many different situations and types of people. We cannot be highly structured and doctrinaire."

Because of the numbers of people retiring from park positions in the 1990s, Snyder thinks that there should be some openings in park work throughout the decade. He suggests that persons wanting to work in the park service should "get your foot in the door through seasonal jobs or volunteer work. Learn to know people and make yourself indispensable to someone."

After more than twenty years of park work (seventeen in the U.S. Park Service), Snyder says with satisfaction that there is nothing about his job that he dislikes.

See Park Resource Management, page 66.

Interpretive Naturalist
Roy Geiger

"Typically you don't get into interpretation unless you have a natural gift for gab and communication," says Roy Geiger, leaning back in his chair in his compact office. Coordinator of the education center and volunteer programs at the National Wildlife Federation's Laurel Ridge Center in Vienna, Virginia, since 1985, Geiger exemplifies the type of person he describes.

"Interpretive naturalists must be 'people persons' who can survive constant interruptions," Geiger adds. "Our principal job is to understand the jargon of the scientists and resource people and distill their information into language that the public understands."

After obtaining a bachelor of science degree in biology with an emphasis in wildlife, Geiger took a seasonal job as an environmental interpretive technician with the Bureau of Parks in Pennsylvania. He found a full-time position with a consulting firm working on contract with the Environmental Protection Agency. This job used his wildlife biology background, but Geiger declares that "living and working in a cubicle and pushing paper got old real fast." So he began working with the Wildlife Federation, initially in a labor maintenance position. "Because of my background as an interpretive naturalist, the job title quickly changed to assistant naturalist," says Geiger—and so did his job.

Geiger's expertise in raptors, or birds of prey, made him a natural choice for a special tour throughout the United States with a live bald eagle. This national educational tour focused on bald eagles and other endangered species.

Geiger is responsible for all the educational activities at the Laurel Ridge Center—a blend of traditional nature center operations, visitors' center, and conference center that accommodates approximately thirty-nine thousand visitors annually. Geiger had a staff of three until budget cuts left him with one staff person and a very active corps of about seventy volunteers who help maintain the program.

According to Geiger, "Most naturalists don't stay on the front lines of interpretation for a long time. To survive and make a decent salary, they work into management." In his management position, Geiger spends very little time working outdoors, which had been an initial attraction to this career. He now trains the teacher-naturalist volunteers to do the field naturalist work. "I've moved more into the role of supervisory mentor," he says.

"We see an increase of public interest in environmental concerns," he points out, "so I think there will continue to be a need for naturalists." Nevertheless, he advises persons who are just entering the field to consider work with environmental consulting firms or as a volunteer to maintain skills and make contacts while they look for a naturalist position.

Geiger likes being an educator and interpreting nature, the environment, and conservation issues to the public— "seeing the light bulbs go on," as he puts it. "I also thoroughly enjoy the personal and professional contacts that I have in this field. I can call people across the country for advice in developing new programs."

"Probably the major thing that I dislike about the position is the bureaucracy," he concludes. "It can be very difficult." Geiger says that many interpretive naturalists are free spirits who find it onerous to have to "dot all the i's, cross the t's, and put everything into the proper proposal form. But it is possible," he adds with a twinkle in his eyes, "to turn the bureaucracy into a game and see how you can beat it or make it work for you."

See Interpretation, page 66.

Fisheries Biologist
Bill Bradshaw

One typical position in fish and wildlife management is that of the fisheries biologist. "Biologists often plan, conduct, and report on studies about fish and fish habitat," says Bill Bradshaw, fisheries biologist with the Fish Division of the Wyoming State Game and Fish Department. "They also get involved in developing regulations, coordinating activities with other agencies or public groups, fisheries resource protection activities, and fish stocking."

Bradshaw works in the field from April through the summer collecting technical information. "I work with the instream flow crew, which determines the amount of water needed to maintain or improve a fishery system," he explains. "When I'm out collecting data, I may drive all day to get to a remote location because my job is statewide and I go all over the state. There I will collect hydraulic information for perhaps three or four days. In the winter, when I work in the office, I use this information to develop reports. It may take years to work out one project, especially if there are political considerations, such as negotiations with different government departments or agencies."

Bradshaw became a fisheries biologist by both "design and default." His original intention was to work in aquaculture (growing fish for market production), and he got a bachelor's degree in that field. "After an internship for the Washington State Department of Fisheries and several jobs, I decided to return to school for a master of science in fisheries instead of marine biology or aquaculture."

Specialized information required for his job includes knowledge of ecology, fish habitat needs, and hydraulics, especially stream hydraulics. Bradshaw adds, "Familiarity with computer models is also important. Some of these special skills I learned on the job—for example, the computer model.

"Writing and verbal communications skills are essential,

because we spend a lot of time writing reports, as well as dealing with coworkers, state agencies, and the public."

Curiosity and the ability to get along with people are two important personality traits for this career. "I spend a lot of time camping out or in hotels with other people," says Bradshaw. "If you don't get along with the person you are working with, even though you may like the setting, the job can be drudgery. We also deal with the public and with persons in other state agencies. Curiosity is important because, as a trained scientist, I work at solving problems. Persons who get into management positions must be continually asking questions. This is a constantly evolving type of position."

Bradshaw believes the outlook for this type of work is good: "There are fairly many jobs, many of which are related to federal funding—usually a five-year allocation. The number will probably continue to grow."

For persons interested in this career, Bradshaw advises, "In looking for jobs be persistent. Get temporary jobs even if this means that you move around. It's important to get experience and meet people. Employment experience is a different kind of educational experience. Keep an open mind and try to have a varied background. Flexibility in outlook and in the approach to solving problems is important."

The work does have a down side. Bradshaw cites as drawbacks the low pay and "the conservative political climate, which sometimes leads to disparaging or negative remarks about being a state employee." Further, he admits that "all of the travel in the summertime does get old." But he sums it up this way: "Overall, I like my job much more than I dislike it."

See Fish and Wildlife Management, page 67.

Forest Supervisor
Wendy Herrett

How did a landscape architect get to be a forester? "I got here by an unusual route," admits Wendy Herrett, forest supervisor for the Siuslaw National Forest in Corvallis, Oregon. "But landscape architecture is one of the paths to an administrative position in the U.S. Forest Service."

Herrett says she became interested in landscape architecture because, "Mountains and the outdoors have always been very attractive to me and I love to garden. Landscape architecture meshed my love of plants and the outdoors with design."

After completing a five-year bachelor's program in landscape architecture, Herrett obtained a job with the U.S. Forest Service. She has held a variety of positions during her twenty-one years with the Forest Service. As a landscape architect, she worked in the regional office in Portland and in two forests: Mount Hood National Forest in Oregon and Routt National Forest in Colorado. Her work included designing campgrounds, reducing the visible impact of timber activities in the forests, and training employees to be sensitive to the visual qualities of the scenery.

After six years as a landscape architect, Herrett began her move into management as resource assistant in Black Hills National Park in South Dakota. She spent several years as district ranger at the White River National Forest in Colorado before she moved to the legislative affairs staff in the Forest Service's Washington, D.C., office. Her responsibilities there included tracking legislation, writing testimonies, preparing and accompanying witnesses to hearings, and assisting members of congress in drafting bills. After leaving Washington, she spent four years as deputy forest supervisor at the Mount Hood National Forest before assuming her present position.

As the forest supervisor, Herrett is in charge of administering all activities authorized by congress, including camping, fisheries enhancement, special projects, trail maintenance and construction, and law enforcement. Her planning and managing functions include coordinating with other agencies, involvement with the public, and seeing that funds are spent within congressional boundaries. She supervises approximately 520 employees, five districts, and a Job Corps center, which provides vocational and educational skills.

Herrett says a sense of humor is essential in her job. "You shouldn't take yourself too seriously. You must be able to respond positively to criticism. Integrity is also important. You should care about the people you are trying to serve and about the land you are trying to protect. Your job is to mesh the needs of people with the desire to protect the land."

As an administrator she spends a lot of time in meetings. "When I am in the field now, I deal mostly with employees rather than with projects," she explains. "I deal with personnel, disciplinary problems, hiring, resource issues, and decisions. It can be stressful, especially now, when more emphasis is placed on fewer resources. The job used to be simpler." She adds, regretfully, "I have worked less in the outdoors as I have moved up to higher positions."

Nevertheless, she likes her career. "It is rewarding when you come to a mutually acceptable solution of a controversy with a group of people," she says. "I like seeing the public enjoy their experience on the land and with the employees. It is fun to see the land. What I don't like is controversy; people can be nasty."

Herrett enjoys working with the Forest Service "because it exposes you to different points of view from both coworkers and the public. To work here one must be open to change and able to listen to more than one point of view. Solutions must be found where possible."

The ability to work with people is essential in forest management, which, Herrett points out, is not strictly a science. "It is important to be in touch with our feelings. Our publics express values based on their feelings, and we need to be able to relate to them and truly understand them so we can honestly consider what they are telling us when we make decisions.

"The career is cyclical and very competitive. With less land available now, timber jobs are not increasing. Jobs for foresters seemed to be on a downward trend for a while. Where there is an increase is in recreation and in wildlife and fish biology."

Herrett has this suggestion for those interested in this career: "Make sure you like working with people. Remember you are dealing with feelings and value systems, not facts. Be as flexible as possible in where you go and what you try, especially to get hired initially."

See Forestry, page 70.

Certified Landscape Architect
Wade Weaver

"I love the activity. There are times when the work is constant and I put in sixty-hour weeks. There is a lot of variety. I've worked with numerous forms of construction, from highways and industrial projects to residential sites, regional malls, shopping centers, and large office parks to a mine reclamation project." Wade Weaver's enthusiasm for his work in landscape architecture is apparent.

"I don't think there's anything that I really dislike about my job," he says candidly. Weaver, who works for L.B.A., Limited, in Fairfax, Virginia, does admit that dealing with personal preferences and personality differences between professionals can be a challenge, but he adds quickly that this is found in every field.

Because the finished appearance is a good promotional tool, landscape architects are involved in the early planning for a project. Many times, however, the basic project is essentially laid out before the landscape architect is called in. At that point, according to Weaver, "You look at what is developed on the base sheets and formulate what the client and the architect are looking for and what should be done considering the various jurisdictions involved. Local zoning and state laws such as the canopy law [areas of the site that must be shaded by trees] must be taken into consideration."

Weaver indicates that the work can be very involved. "Rules and regulations are a hodgepodge of numerous directives. These are established by each county or region and have become very technical in the last few years." After graduation and required years of work in the field, landscape architects take a certification of licensure examination in the state where they work. Weaver is certified as a landscape architect in the state of Virginia.

The actual work of the landscape architect—the finishing touches—comes at the end of a project. The landscape architect must then take into account construction problems and a budget that may have been reappropriated. "At that point, with less money than earlier anticipated, the architect may have to revise the plans drawn up before the project was begun," Weaver explains.

Weaver spent a total of seven years in preparation for his career. He initially spent two years each in civil and architectural engineering. Then he picked up additional credits in parks and recreation and in fine arts while completing a four-year landscape architecture degree program in three years.

Weaver readily admits that much of his work goes beyond the scope of traditional landscape architects because of his well-rounded education. "My education has been an asset in my current projects, and it has carried me in a recession. I've outlasted people who had more seniority. I'm still here on a work force that, because of the economy, has shrunk from 140 to 20 people." Weaver suggests that to weather economic downturns, a landscape architect should have a varied background; this will also provide more flexibility in job options.

His varied education and experience may also account for what Weaver calls his "forte in finding solutions to problems created by other landscape installation firms—for example, when the plant mix, while it presented a nice collage of colors and types, didn't succeed because it wasn't adaptable to the soil and shade conditions and the moisture restraints." He adds, "Many people think that a landscape architect is a gardener, but the work goes beyond that."

He sees the potential for the field to expand, especially considering the current focus on the environment and environmental problems. "I'm heavily into environmental issues right now. The landscape architect can take man-made features such as those used in stormwater management and turn them into a more natural setting. The work can help to improve water quality, facilitating erosion control measures, and assist in the preservation of vegetation while improving maintenance operations for the site. It can be beneficial for the environment and for the resale or further development of the project."

Weaver suggests that landscape architecture is a good career for those who have an interest in nature and the environment and are "productive, energetic persons." He adds, "I would say general experience—being around construction, plant material, and so on—gives you a more rounded approach to the work. The education is important and beneficial, but I think you have to have something more: a desire to help people and nature."

The chief personality traits Weaver feels are necessary for this career are flexibility and congeniality. These are important, he explains, "because you have to work with other professionals." Other important qualities Weaver cites include being somewhat aggressive and willing to promote what you think is best. Landscape architects need to listen to the client, understand the needs, and pull the different concepts together, meshing and blending them. A person should have a well-rounded background and know where to get specialized information when it is needed.

"You will also look at how the thing fits together and how you will dovetail all the different aspects. Then you must disguise many things, such as utilities. Much of your work is buried," Weaver admits, laughing. "Many times no one recognizes the work, but you're the first one to be blamed when something doesn't look good."

See Landscape Architecture, page 75.

5

*"We travel together, passengers on a little spaceship
dependent on its vulnerable supplies of air and soil: all
committed for our safety to its security and peace, preserved from annihilation only by the care, the work, and I will
say the love we give our fragile craft."*

Adlai Stevenson

Environmental Sciences

The sciences that focus on our environment—the environmental
sciences—provide some work opportunities in the outdoors. The
major fields in this category are geography, geology, meteorology,
and oceanography. Each of these fields contains subspecialties.

Environmental scientists study the history, makeup, and characteristics of the atmosphere, surface, and core of the earth. Generally they study nonliving things, although there are some notable
exceptions to this rule. Geographers, for example, study people and
how they relate to their environment. Research is very important in
these fields, as is the ability to apply the information gained in a
practical manner.

Geography

Salary Range: professors with a doctorate, $21,600 to
$25,900; in private industry, $28,100 to $38,900

Educational Requirements: minimum of a bachelor's
degree, with graduate study an asset; master's needed
for teaching in two-year colleges; doctorate needed for
top government and private-industry positions and
teaching in universities

Employment Outlook: good

Geography is both a natural science and a social science. That is, it studies both people and their environment and helps to draw connections between the cultural and physical worlds. Although the work of geographers is directly related to the outdoors, a great deal of it takes place indoors.

Some topics of concern to geographers are acid rain, nuclear war, hazardous waste, low-income housing, and the growth of world population. With better international communications and more interdependence among world nations, the geographer's expertise in analyzing global patterns should be increasingly drawn upon.

The two essential questions that geographers ask as they study are *where* and *why:* Where are things situated, and why are they situated at that location? The first calls for a descriptive answer and the second for an analytic response. Geographers have traditionally gathered data through field observation—from the ground, balloons, aircraft, and satellites. This data provided the basis for making maps, the basic tools geographers use in presenting information. But with the current explosion of technology, geographers are able to use new methodologies, such as computers, in collecting, analyzing, and presenting data.

Within geography are three different fields, each of which has its own distinct subfields. Physical, or environmental, geography includes the subfields of climatology, biogeography, and geomorphology; human geography includes the subfields of urban, population, political, and cultural geography; and technical geography includes the subfields of cartography, remote sensing, photogrammetry, and geographic information systems.

As a discipline, geography provides students with a body of theory and methodologies leading to an analytic technique that can be used for various occupations. Almost one-quarter of all professional geographers today are employed in government at the federal, state, and local levels and in federal agencies, the armed forces, and international organizations. Few are employed under the job title of geographer; many titles fall into this category, including cartographer, geographic analyst, map curator, land officer, international economist, intelligence officer, and soil conservationist.

Other geographers work in private business, which is increasingly using their skills. These positions involve industrial location analysis, market research, and transportation design and planning. Regional and metropolitan planning is another field for geographers that is developing quite rapidly. And publishers of maps, atlases, textbooks, encyclopedias, and news and travel magazines often employ geographers as writers and editors. Geographers also teach in universities and colleges.

See Profile, page 102.

Geology

Salary Range: starting with a bachelor's degree between $20,500 and $22,700; with a master's, about $27,000; with experience and a doctorate, $51,900

Educational Requirements: those with just a bachelor's degree will face stiff competition; for research, an advanced degree is required; for teaching in a four-year college, a doctorate is required

Employment Outlook: fair

Geologists study the earth's crust by looking at the structure, history, and composition of the upper layers and at the physical processes that change the earth. Many occupations in geology are involved in the exploration of the earth for resources such as oil and various minerals.

There are many different, often interrelated, subfields in geology.

Economic geologists help in locating and developing natural resources such as minerals and fossil fuels. *Engineering geologists* study sites for the construction of airfields, bridges, buildings, dams, highways, tunnels, and other structures and work out geological engineering problems. *Environmental geologists* focus on pollution, urban development, land use, and resource development problems. *Geochemists* study the type and location of chemical elements in rocks and minerals. *Geochronologists* determine the age of rocks by calculating the rate at which certain radioactive elements decay. *Glaciologists* study the types, movement, causes, and effects of glaciers.

Hydrologists and *hydrogeologists* focus on surface and underground water supplies. *Marine geologists* study the ocean and the continental shelf. *Mineralogists* study and classify the origins, composition, and properties of minerals. *Mining geologists* work in tandem with engineers to develop mines for the safe recovery of minerals. *Paleobotanists* and *paleontologists* identify, study, and classify fossils. *Petrologists* study the origins and composition of rocks. *Planetary geologists* examine the moon, planets, and solar system. *Sedimentologists* examine the characteristics, movement, and origins of sedimentary deposits. *Stratigraphers* study the mineral and fossil content as well as the thickness, shape, and distribution of layered rocks. *Structural geologists* investigate rock formations and layers and the forces producing or changing them. *Volcanologists* examine the geologic phenomena related to volcanic activity.

Jobs in geology are available with a variety of employers. Although petroleum exploration was depressed in the latter part of the 1980s, the need in this area may increase in the 1990s because of the growing world demand for oil. Some of the larger companies are selectively hiring staff for future exploration needs. Petroleum exploration work in the future will be very challenging as it becomes more sophisticated and highly computerized. It will also be in increasingly remote and difficult locations such as deep in the oceans and in arctic, desert, and jungle areas.

Another employer of geologists is the mining industry. This industry experiences boom and bust cycles, and the competition for jobs is keen. If you decide to work in exploration or mining geology, make sure that you have a strong interest in these fields. This will help carry you through the bust periods.

Exploration geologists work to discover mineral deposits, and mining geologists work to turn a mineral deposit into profit. These jobs call for dedication and travel, flexibility in location and relocation, and the willingness to terminate favorite projects because of economic reasons. If you aren't willing to make these concessions, consider other employers, such as academic, government, or research organizations, whose work emphasizes applying science to the study and understanding of ore deposits. The field experienced a boom in the early 1990s, mostly in gold mining and exploration in Nevada, but the future is not at all certain.

Other major employers of geologists are the federal, state, and local governments. In the federal government, the largest employer by far is the U.S. Geological Survey in the Department of the Interior. Other Department of the Interior bureaus hiring geoscientists are the Bureaus of Land Management and Reclamation and Mines and the Minerals Management Service.

Geoscientists are also hired by the Departments of Agriculture, Defense, Commerce, and Energy, and the Environmental Protection Agency. Considering the major water problems already facing the United States, it is not surprising that the U.S. Geological Survey had a great demand for hydrologists at the end of the 1980s. At the state level, the largest number of geological positions is with state geological surveys. Other state and local agencies tend to have more geologist positions in the areas of environmental regulation.

Although some academic employment opportunities in the geological sciences do exist, this is not an area of major employment.

Consulting opportunities in the geoscience-related areas of water resources, hazardous waste management, and process engineering look very promising. The best background for consulting work is a major in hydrogeology, geochemistry, civil engineering, or sanitary engineering, or a well-rounded study of geology. In addition to their technical knowledge, graduates should be aware of policy and institutional issues, which can be learned through business management, economics, law, and planning courses.

Consulting work is subject to change, and consultants need to follow the changing market. For example, in the middle 1980s there was a great demand for consultants in the construction of dams and nuclear power plants. The emphasis in the early 1990s was on water resources and hazardous waste disposal and control. To adapt to changing market needs, flexibility and a variety of skills will be most valuable in the consulting business. Continuing education and the ability to change one's focus are also essential.

See Profile, page 104.

Meteorology

Salary Range: depends on education and the employer; federal government jobs from $14,000 to $30,200; supervisors in private industry up to $97,000

Educational Requirements: in the armed services, meteorologists receive on-the-job training; otherwise, a bachelor's degree is the minimum for federal jobs, and a master's or doctorate is needed for teaching and research

Employment Outlook: very good—the field is expected to increase faster than the average; jobs are more likely for people with advanced degrees and with the National Weather Service

The science of meteorology is concerned with observing, describing, understanding, forecasting, and possibly controlling the behavior of the atmosphere. The best known meteorologist is the person who conveys weather forecasts to a local area—usually known as the weather forecaster. Meteorology careers, however, are not limited to weather forecasting. TV meteorologists make up only a small percentage of the field: Only about one out of every eight meteorologists works on television.

Meteorological research is conducted in an effort to gain more understanding of the atmosphere. To do this, mathematical models, computers, and technical developments such as Doppler radars and satellites are used. A major goal is improving skills in predicting changes in weather patterns to improve the quality of forecasting. Applied research goes a step farther; there, the findings of basic research for specific functions such as designing aircraft, conserving water resources, controlling air pollution, and improving forecasting are used.

Meteorology also influences planning and design in engineering. The product must be able to withstand the ravages of the local environment. Whether it is bridges, highways, or buildings that are being constructed, information on the atmosphere is an important factor to consider.

Weather forecasters play a major role in the economy of the country. Their information influences decisions about crop planting and harvesting, air transportation, and the protection of cities against weather hazards and pollution, among other things. Also affected are decisions made by the general public regarding travel and vacation plans. Some specialized areas are flood and hurricane forecasting and forecasting for local highway system personnel to help them determine when to salt or plow roads.

The major employer of meteorologists nationally is the U.S. government, specifically the National Oceanic and Atmospheric Administration. Private industry, especially consulting and research firms, also use meteorologists. Consulting meteorologists help companies solve such problems as determining smokestack height or solar exposure.

Another career possibility is teaching. Meteorology, or atmospheric sciences, as it is sometimes called, is now taught at many universities and colleges throughout the country. Meteorology teaching jobs are more plentiful in the environmental sciences, an important area of study today. Research positions are also available at universities.

A bachelor's degree in meteorology is the minimum education necessary for meteorology jobs. Persons wanting to get into research will need more education. Meteorology may be combined with another discipline, such as agriculture, astronomy, or civil, environmental, or electrical engineering, to open the possibility of an interdisciplinary career.

See Profile, page 107.

Oceanography

Salary Range: starting between $17,300 and $27,000; average $32,400 with experience; in private industry, between $56,000 and $64,800

Educational Requirements: minimum of a bachelor's

degree, although graduate training will give the best advancement potential; a doctorate is required for many research positions and college teaching
Employment Outlook: fair

The oceanographer uses the basic sciences in studying the oceans and the ocean environment. Oceanography is an interdisciplinary science that studies the biological, physical, chemical, and geological processes of the ocean. The biological oceanographer studies marine life from microscopic forms to the blue whale. The chemical oceanographer looks at the chemical composition and chemical reactions of the ocean's water. The geological oceanographer is concerned with mineral deposits on the seafloor and tectonic forces that influence ocean basins. And the physical oceanographer examines the motions of the seas, such as currents and waves, and the density, salinity, and temperature of the water.

Oceanographers share a commitment to research and to put to good use the results of research projects. Some oceanographers go out to sea on research vessels to collect data, while others employ data from satellites or use computer modeling.

The government is a major employer of oceanographers, but private industries, consulting firms, and educational institutions also have many positions. The academic setting involves both teaching and research.

Resources
Geography
Careers in Geography, Geography as a Discipline, Geography: Today's Career for Tomorrow, and *Why Geography?* (pamphlets), Association of American Geographers, 1710 Sixteenth Street, N.W., Washington, DC 20009-3198 (202-234-1450).

Geology
Careers in Geology (pamphlet), American Geological Institute, 4220 King Street, Alexandria, VA 22302 (703-379-2480).

Future Employment Opportunities in the Geological Sciences (pamphlet), The Geological Society of America, 3300 Penrose Place, P.O. Box 9140, Boulder, CO 80301 (303-447-2020).

Meteorology
The Changing Atmosphere: Challenges and Opportunities and *The Challenge of Meteorology* (pamphlets), American Meteorological Society, 45 Beacon Street, Boston, MA 02108.

Oceanography
Careers in Oceanography, American Geophysical Union, 2000 Florida Avenue, N.W., Washington, DC 20009.

Careers in Oceanography (a different pamphlet), Oregon State University, Hatfield Marine Science Center Aquarium, Extension Sea Grant Program, 2030 S. Marine Science Drive, Newport, OR 97365 (503-867-3011 ext. 228).

Training and Careers in Marine Science (booklet), International Oceanographic Foundation, 3979 Rickenbacker Causeway, Virginia Key, Miami, FL 33149.

Geographer
Linda Higgs

How did geography major Linda Higgs wind up working for Paul C. Rizzo Associates, Inc., an engineering consulting firm in Monroeville, Pennsylvania? Higgs credits her success to timing and her versatile geography skills.

After graduating from college with a bachelor's degree in geography, she sent her résumé in response to an ad for an environmental engineer, thinking the company might be able to use someone with her background. At that time the company, which was hoping to establish the first hazardous waste landfill in Pennsylvania, did indeed want someone with her background and she was hired.

"I was able to define my own job," Higgs says. She also chose her job title—assistant project geographer. The staff consists mainly of engineers, but has a strong strain of geologists and one geographer—Higgs.

Higgs works in the hazardous waste division of the company—the other two divisions are dams/hydro and power—investigating locations for landfill and hazardous waste sites. She explains: "I do the preliminary work. Then the geologists take over the project and do a soil analysis, and the engineers complete the design."

When making an environmental assessment of a site, Higgs investigates the physical description, the soil, the topography, accessibility, geological features, the local population, historical sites, and any local endangered species by using topographical quadrangles, maps, aerial photography, and mine maps. She also contacts governmental and local groups such as historical commissions and fish and game commissions, checks state regulations, and obtains permission from the contiguous landowners. Although Higgs spends about four weeks a year outdoors, most of her time is spent indoors.

"I enjoy the variety of the job—there is no such thing as a typical day," she says happily. "My job is different from everyone else's in the company, and I'm not stuck in one position. I have a lot of interaction with clients and regulatory agencies that most of the others don't have."

Before she decided on a geography major, Higgs tried out biochemistry and mathematics/business. Although they didn't work out as majors for her, Higgs says with a laugh, "On this job I have used all of my courses." Higgs has taken continuing education courses in wetlands design and environmental auditing to keep her skills sharp. "I want to keep my skills and knowledge current," she explains.

For her job Higgs says it is important to be creative, have good research skills, know how to use computer indexes, and be willing to look for information. "I need to be friendly, especially in my phone contacts with regulatory people, and very flexible. Because very few companies use geographers, I had to be willing to do anything until I established what I could do for the company. I've made a specialty of handling things that no one else wants to do, making myself indispensable." Higgs uses her writing skills for reports and letters.

Higgs enjoys her job: "I am basically my own boss and I can keep myself busy for months. I like being independent and setting my own schedule." Sometimes she wishes, however, that people would know what she does and that she could do more work relating to geography.

Higgs says a degree in geography opens up lots of opportunities—"I just happened to get into environmental engineering." Her recommendation to other geography graduates: "Don't shut out any options. Look everywhere. Be prepared to sell yourself and tell a company what you can do for them."

See Geography, page 93.

Geologist
Norma Biggar

"Although geologists have the reputation of being loners, my job as a consultant is pretty communicative," says Norma Biggar with a smile. "It involves a lot of teamwork."

As senior geologist and associate with Woodward-Clyde Consultants, a large consulting firm headquartered in Denver, Colorado, Biggar specializes in seismic hazards in their Oakland, California, office. Located some sixty miles from the epicenter of the 1989 Loma Prieta earthquake and a mile from the site of the double-decker highway that collapsed during that quake, the firm is well situated for dealing with earthquakes.

Biggar describes her job as a balancing act: "I conduct the technical studies on some projects and manage others, review work by others in the company, develop technical approaches for projects, develop budgets and write proposals, and occasionally give presentations to clients. No two days are ever alike."

To determine if there have been any major earthquakes in an area during the last ten thousand or so years, Biggar searches for the landforms unique to faults along which shallow and moderate- to large-magnitude earthquakes occur. To do this, she first examines published geologic maps and talks with other geologists who may have mapped faults in the area. Then she studies aerial photographs and may do aerial over-flights from an altitude of about 3,000 feet for a firsthand view of ground features. Features of particular interest are then investigated on the ground. Each of these steps narrows the scope of the examination. "If a feature is suspected to be an active fault, we excavate one or more trenches—three feet wide and ten to fifteen feet deep—across it with a backhoe and log the fault features seen in the trench walls," she explains.

"The objectives are to define the fault zone and the style of faulting, and to learn when and how frequently the most recent earthquakes have occurred along the fault." Engineers use the data she gathers to deal with the perceived seismic risk when designing structures to withstand earthquakes.

Biggar chose geology after enrolling in a geology class to complete college course requirements. "I found the course very interesting and the material very familiar. The fact that the prof was a woman may have had some influence on my interest," she adds candidly. "I like geology because it is a very interdisciplinary science and integrates biology, chemistry, physics, and rock mechanics into understanding the earth processes."

For the consulting work she does, Biggar says a master's degree or at least some graduate study is necessary. On-the-job experience is also important. Her own credentials include a bachelor's degree in earth science and a master's in geology. She joined Woodward-Clyde nineteen years ago on a summer job and never left.

Biggar says that an ability to think in three dimensions is important for geologists—they must visualize the earth's structures both within a hundred feet of the ground surface and to a depth of several miles. "We use multiple working hypotheses and visualize various scenarios; one needs to have an open mind in evaluating the situation and looking at it from many angles." Technical and report writing abilities are also important, and a knowledge of computer applications is becoming more necessary.

Consultants need to be very flexible. "You must be able to deal with clients under tough time constraints who change their minds and want something else. You need to respond rapidly to change."

"I enjoy the novelty and the changeability of my work—and the opportunities to learn something about totally new areas," Biggar says. "Dealing with earthquakes also keeps me humble. I am frequently reminded of the insignificance of human activities when they are compared with the power unleashed in a large earthquake.

"I guess I dislike the same things I like," she adds with a chuckle. "It is difficult to create a realistic schedule several weeks or months in the future. While the flexibility requirements and travel can be challenging and fun, they are also disruptive to personal life. I have to help some of our clients, who aren't familiar with the complexities of the work, understand the amount of time it may take to obtain the product [report] they desire."

Biggar doesn't get outside as much now as she used to, but last year she spent two months outside on a field assignment and in a recent week she was out six days. "People on the staff level do most of the fun work," she says ruefully. "The amount of time outside and the quality of that outside time depend on the project."

Biggar says job availability for geologists will continue. Many nonpetroleum jobs are driven by regulatory compliance issues, which are becoming more pervasive in our society. The hot spots now for geologists are in hazardous waste. In fact, Biggar has just been transferred to Woodward-Clyde's office in Las Vegas to work on site characterization of a proposed high-level nuclear waste repository.

Biggar advises would-be geologists to get at least a bachelor's degree and study a broad range of topics, including hydrology, and develop investigative and writing skills through experience. She also recommends taking the geologic field trips available from different organizations to network and learn of local geologic issues and the work that others are doing. "Then I suggest finding someone who's enthusiastic about your field of interest and working with her," she adds.

See Geology, page 95.

Meteorologist
Ken Rancourt

"Meteorology was a good major for me, because I like being outdoors and I like computers and mathematics," explains Ken Rancourt, staff meteorologist at the Mount Washington Observatory in New Hampshire.

A private, nonprofit research organization, the observatory is perched atop New Hampshire's highest mountain, Mount Washington, 6,288 feet above sea level. Rancourt points out that it is "strictly a weather observatory. We do not forecast the weather."

As part of the contract to provide accurate weather reports for the U.S. Weather Service, on-duty observatory staffers must take five to ten minutes every three hours to observe the weather, checking on such things as cloud cover and density. One of Rancourt's major functions is to handle the research that goes on at the station. Because Mount Washington experiences "the world's worst weather," it is a prime location for research on cold regions. The observatory contracts with various organizations, such as the U.S. Army, 3M, and the National Weather Service, to carry on research.

Staff members spend a week at a time on the mountain, from Wednesday to Wednesday. Two to three persons are on duty at all times, working eight- to ten-hour shifts. When the new crew comes up with food and the mail, there is a shift meeting and then the off-duty shift leaves for the week.

A typical day begins at about 5:30 A.M. "The morning person gets the forecast from the weather service and an updated weather map and does the six o'clock observation," Rancourt details. "We do several taped radio broadcasts and a couple of live radio shows to disseminate the weather for the northern part of New Hampshire. On the live show, a five-minute broadcast, we talk about weather conditions at the summit and at the station at the base of the mountain; then we briefly discuss the weather map, what's happening in the general area, and the local forecast."

Rancourt says that because the main research goes on in the winter, the only reason to go outdoors in the summer is the weather observation every three hours. He adds, "You do get sort of cramped once in a while and go outside anyway. In the wintertime we may go out as frequently as once an hour. That means getting dressed in full weather regalia, taking measurements and pictures, or doing whatever is required by contract."

As this is a relatively small observatory, with four basic staff members, everyone is required to do everything, Rancourt explains. "Both the museum manager and I do radio shows. He fixes the oil furnaces when they go out, and we all handle things such as propane problems. Many people do many things, and that's why the place works."

This brings Rancourt to a misconception he wants to correct. "I know a lot of people think that you must be lonely if you work on the summit of Mount Washington. We had twenty-one for supper on Saturday night. It's hard to be lonely when you're washing dishes for twenty-one people," he laughs, "especially since we let our guests help with the work. In the summer our crew swells to ten, with state park rangers and a night cleanup person."

Rancourt started college as an aerospace engineering major but "read the handwriting on the wall" when Boeing had their first big layoff in the late 1960s. He switched to meteorology after hands-on summer experience for the division of meteorology at Iowa University, which "really sparked my interest." Rancourt has both a bachelor's and a master's degree in meteorology.

Failing to find a meteorology job right after graduation, Rancourt worked for a construction company for a while, then moved to a company that supplied radar equipment to schools. In this job he combined knowledge of both electronics and meteorology. He has been at Mount Washington for twelve years now, and finds his construction knowledge a plus because, with the difficulty of winter travel, it isn't always easy to get a carpenter or plumber, and the ability to fix things oneself is important.

"On the job I'm more of a support person, even though I have degrees in meteorology," he says. "But it's important to have someone with my experience here so that we can help set up effective research."

It is essential for a meteorologist to be able to use computers and work with statistical analysis. Rancourt adds, "You have to be personable and like communicating with the general public. It is also important to be able to work with a team. And a background in the physical sciences is essential."

Rancourt does find the week-on, week-off schedule difficult but confides, "I think I'm pretty lucky. I really do like my job, and that makes this schedule easier to handle."

He cautions that his job is not typical of many meteorological positions, but, he asserts, "One thing that is typical of all meteorologists is that we enjoy watching the world around us—clouds, as well as the life around us, the lichens, the mosses, and the animals. Most meteorologists are interested in the out-of-doors."

See Meteorology, page 98.

"**A** *problem well stated is a problem half solved.*"
Charles F. Kettering

6

Engineering

The profession of engineering goes back to the earliest times of recorded history. Persons who built irrigation canals, palaces, temples, roads, baths, aqueducts, and other structures that met the needs of others were called engineers. In military preparation and campaigns, engineers built forts and machines of war.

Engineers work to find solutions to specific practical problems confronting society. They take abstract scientific principles and technical knowledge and translate these into practical applications in the process of designing solutions to problems.

As our society changes and the problems we confront change, the field of engineering is also changing. Additionally, new materials and processes are enabling engineers to use more advanced technologies, and the profession is growing in importance.

There are at least fifty engineering specialties, most of which stem from what are considered the "classical" branches of engineering. Because engineers work to solve problems, new subfields are constantly being developed as new types of problems emerge. The following are the fields generally considered to be the classical branches.

Aeronautical engineers research, develop, design, and test vehicles, both manned and unmanned, that operate above or below the surface of the earth.

Agricultural engineers are concerned with developing, maintaining, and using farm equipment and buildings, as well as efficiently raising crops and taking care of the needs of farm animals.

Bioengineers apply the technology of other engineering fields to the health and comfort of human beings. This is the most recent addition to the classical branches.

Ceramic engineers work with developing and applying materials, either natural or synthetic, made from inorganic matter whose value results from high-temperature processing. Some of the products are pottery, lasers, semiconductors, and protective shields for space travel.

Chemical engineers design, develop, and apply the processes that change raw materials in their chemical construction and material shape. Some of the products are fuels, fertilizers, plastics, and paper.

Civil engineers are concerned with the building of structures that relate to community life, such as houses, office and public buildings, highways, railroads, bridges, tunnels, and dams. This is the oldest classical engineering branch.

Electrical engineers work in electronics, power, and information processing. Computer engineering, which may soon be considered a separate branch, now comes under electrical. Electrical engineering is one of the largest engineering branches in the number of practitioners.

Industrial engineers are involved with the cost and construction of goods. This engineer works mostly in plants, coordinating personnel, materials, and machinery and deciding the best way to use each of these in order to produce the most economical product.

Mechanical engineers are concerned chiefly with the planning and operating of machines that produce and relay power.

Metallurgical engineers, unlike others, are more involved with matter than with machines, power, or structures.

Agricultural Engineering

Salary Range: starting at about $27,800; with a master's degree, $28,100 to $37,800; with a doctorate, $45,400 to $54,000

Educational Requirements: college

Employment Outlook: fair

Career opportunities in agricultural engineering vary widely both in type of work and in location. Agricultural engineers are involved in all facets of food production, processing, marketing, and distribution.

There are four main areas in agricultural engineering: product design, which mainly involves designing specific products such as machinery or structures; systems engineering, which includes irrigation equipment, environmental, electrical, microprocessor control, and farmstead types of engineering; resource engineering, which involves water quality and management; and process engineering, which pertains to food and crop processing and crop production.

The agricultural engineering graduate may be involved in developing machines to make work easier; controlling pollution; preserving and protecting dwindling land, air, and water resources; developing new food products; and increasing food productivity. Other possibilities in this subfield include work in quality control, consulting, and sales and management.

Job locations for agricultural engineers vary considerably; they may be in rural areas or in major population centers. Many agricultural engineers work overseas helping developing countries increase agricultural production or assisting with soil and water conservation.

With the increase in world population and the concomitant demand for more food, job opportunities for agricultural engineers will continue to grow.

Civil Engineering

Salary Range: starting between $21,600 and $25,900; average $32,400 to $40,500
Educational Requirements: college plus training
Employment Outlook: very good

Civil engineers design and supervise construction of the physical infrastructure that is necessary for modern life. Among the earlier responsibilities of the civil engineer were the building of bridges, highways, dams, aqueducts for conducting water, and canals. Tunnels, water supply systems, pipelines, and irrigation and sewerage systems are also the concern of the civil engineer. More recently, civil engineers have been occupied in building airports and ballistic missile facilities, space exploration technology, and the control of air and water pollution.

Civil engineers work at building structures that are strong, safe, and in conformation with regulations and building codes. They are involved in surveying the building site, preparing it for construction, and selecting the correct materials. Knowledge of the use of construction equipment, such as bulldozers, power shovels, and cranes, is important. This branch of engineering can be divided into six broad categories: construction, structural, transportation, hydraulics, foundation, and sanitary. Structural engineers are concerned with the analysis of forces and materials and how they interact; they design bridges, subways, large buildings, dams, and piers. Construction engineers coordinate the designs of other engineers, prepare the land, schedule construction, and handle all field supervision. Foundation engineers know how soils behave under stress and give data to the structural engineer to aid in preparing the design. Transportation engineers are concerned with traffic control and flow, as well as designing highways, railroads, waterways, and airports. Sanitary engineers design facilities to provide clean water, dispose of wastes, and control pollution. Hydraulic engineers work with dams, reservoirs, canals, irrigation projects, and water supply systems.

The term *civil engineer* initially meant a builder of civil or domestic structures. Over the years, civil engineering has changed and adjusted as civilization has changed. This flexibility will likely continue, and some of the new specialties may gain in importance and become branches separate from civil engineering.

Civil engineering offers a wide range of career choices, as it is possible to combine any of the various subcategories or specialties into a career that is well suited to the interests of the individual.
See Profile, page 120.

Environmental Engineering

Salary Range: starting at about $32,400 with a bachelor's degree; $36,700 with a master's; and $43,200 with a doctorate

Educational Requirements: college; master's degree and doctorate give advantages in finding better jobs and in advancement

Employment Outlook: excellent

The environmental engineer is involved in environmental protection. The major areas include air pollution control, hazardous waste management, industrial hygiene, public health, toxic materials control, radiation protection, storm water management, land management, wastewater management, solid waste disposal, and water supply.

Environmental engineers can select from a great variety of employers and locations. Organizations employing environmental engineers include industries and private businesses; consulting engineering firms; research firms; government agencies at federal, state, and local levels; testing laboratories; and universities. These employers are located around the world.

Work for environmental engineers can be inside or outside. Typically, the mix will be 25 percent outdoors and 75 percent indoors. There are, however, many jobs where 100 percent of the work is done outdoors. Most positions will be found where there are high concentrations of people, since that is where pollution problems generally occur. Types of jobs include research, design, planning, operating pollution control facilities, working for government regulatory agencies, managing programs, teaching, and working in a professional society.

The best preparation for an environmental engineering career is a degree in environmental, civil, mechanical, or chemical engineering. A master's degree or a doctorate will give a job seeker an edge, since more employers now give preference to candidates with advanced degrees.

The basic components of engineering degrees are math, science, and engineering mechanics courses. And since environmental engineering is involved with people, it is also important to know how individuals and societies function, so students should take humanities courses as well. Writing and speaking skills are important for engineers, and these should be developed both in formal studies and in extracurricular activities. To solve problems, engineers have to communicate well with people, and communications skills can only be learned and perfected by doing.

Jobs for environmental engineers outnumber the candidates for these jobs, so this is a rather secure field to enter. Because the work is constantly changing and conditions and policies change,

ental engineers will likely need to retrain several times in the
a lifetime, so commitment to lifelong learning is important.
Profile, page 122.

Geotechnical Engineering

Salary Range: starting between $21,600 and $25,900;
average $32,400 to $40,500
Educational Requirements: college plus training
Employment Outlook: very good

Geotechnical engineering is a branch of civil engineering. These engineers design and construct structures that are underground, on the ground, or made out of the ground. Tunnels, pipelines, and underground openings are examples of structures constructed underground. Bridges, roadways, dams, wastewater treatment facilities, and landfills are all constructed on the ground; some of these are also made of materials from the ground. Works constructed out of the ground (soil and rock) include dams, canals, highway embankments, and landfills.

For construction on the ground, geotechnical engineers are involved at the beginning of a project. They test to determine soil conditions and movements. For this testing, they will drill to obtain samples of the soil and rocks on the site and will also observe the geology. Based on their laboratory analysis of this information, they then prepare a report recommending the specifications for the type of materials that should be used for each particular type of facility. Monitoring the facility during construction to make certain that their testing was accurate is also an essential part of geotechnical engineering.

Standard training for a geotechnical engineer is a bachelor's degree in civil engineering plus a master's in civil engineering with a geotechnical engineering specialty; few practice geotechnical engineering without the master's degree. A doctorate qualifies one for a specialty within the field, such as earthquake engineering. Geotechnical engineering students take a heavy concentration of geology courses in addition to science and mathematics.

Waste management engineering, a part of geotechnical engineering, is a fast-growing engineering subfield because of the tremendous problems of solid waste management, hazardous waste, and toxic cleanup in this country. Because they often deal with ground or groundwater contamination or landfill sites, geotechnical engineers will continue to provide assistance in solving those problems.

See Profile, page 125.

Petroleum Engineering

Salary Range: starting at about $35,600 with a bachelor's degree; $45,600 with a master's; $66,400 with a doctorate

Educational Requirements: college

Employment Outlook: poor; will improve if the price of oil rises

The petroleum engineer develops and produces energy economically and safely from resources deep inside the earth, sometimes even undersea; these include oil and natural gas, as well as geothermal resources. Because these resources can be studied only from the surface, which may be a mile above the resource, the petroleum engineer has to use modern technologies and many sciences to learn about the deposit and develop it.

Petroleum engineers may specialize in various areas. A drilling engineer chooses necessary equipment for a drilling rig, makes an estimation of the cost, and supervises the entire drilling process. A production engineer uses chemical or mechanical means to maximize production from oil and gas wells already in use. And a reservoir engineer works to find the best method to develop a reservoir of natural energy; these methods may include injecting water, gas, or steam, or using chemical flooding to most economically obtain the natural resources.

Petroleum engineers work indoors or outdoors in settings as different as research laboratories and off-shore drilling rigs. They work at locations all around the world for large integrated oil companies or for companies that only explore and produce petroleum and let other companies refine and sell it. Some positions for petroleum engineers are available with the government at all levels, federal, state, and local. There are teaching and research opportunities at universities. It is also possible to be self-employed as a consultant to companies.

Demand for petroleum engineers is not constant; this industry is subject to many ups and downs. Because there will always be a need for energy, it is likely that there will continue to be openings in this area of engineering. Prospective petroleum engineers should check this out, however, before investing too much time and money in study.

Resources

General

Facts about the Society of Women Engineers, High School Preparation for a Bachelor of Science Degree in Engineering, The Society of Women Engineers Scholarship Program, What Are You Doing for the Rest of Your Life?, Women in Engineering, and *Is Engineering for You?* (pamphlets), Society of Women Engineers, United Engineering Center, Room 305, 345 East 47th Street, New York, NY 10017 (212-705-7855).

Women Engineer, National Executive Committee for Guidance, c/o ABET, 345 East 47th Street, New York, NY 10017.

Agricultural Engineering

Agricultural Engineering: The Place to Be; Agricultural Engineering . . .; The Place to Be; Reader Profile; and *9 Overviews: Industries, Technologies & Professional Challenges* (pamphlets), American Society of Agricultural Engineers, 2950 Niles Road, St. Joseph, MI 49085-9659 (616-429-0300).

Civil Engineering

Is *Civil Engineering for You?* (pamphlet), American Society of Civil Engineers, 345 East 47th Street, New York, NY 10017.

Environmental Engineering

Some career and educational information available from American
   Academy of Environmental Engineers, 130 Holiday Court,
   Suite 100, Annapolis, MD 21401 (301-266-3311).

Geological and Geophysical Engineering

Brochure available from Colorado School of Mines, Golden, CO
   80401.

Petroleum Engineering

Careers in Petroleum Engineering and *Petroleum Engineering: Your
   Future in Energy* (pamphlets), Society of Petroleum Engineers,
   222 Palisades Creek Drive, P.O. Box 833836, Richardson, TX
   75083-3836 (214-669-3377).

Civil Engineer
Dennis McDonough

"Everything is outdoors or outdoor-related activities." Regional engineering supervisor Dennis McDonough exudes enthusiasm as he talks about his job with the Ducks Unlimited (DU) regional office in Jackson, Mississippi. McDonough, who has a bachelor's degree in civil engineering, works as a regional biologist. "We do habitat enhancement," he explains. "We travel to a site in pairs: a biologist and an engineer. There the biologist determines the habitat needed and the engineer comes up with the concept and design to provide that habitat. It's a perfect job."

McDonough previously worked in the DU North Dakota office, where, he says, "We did all nesting or production habitats. This means work with dams, dikes, islands, level ditching, and that type of engineering. We did some fairly deep water impoundment to provide secure water for nesting." In Jackson, DU provides migratory habitats. Now, McDonough relates, "I work with shallow water covering a larger area, but the function is the same. The biologist still determines what is needed for a habitat, and the engineer comes up with the design and structures."

McDonough details his experience: "I spent fourteen years with the U.S. Soil Conservation Service and four years with the Forest Service before I went to work with DU in 1985. With the Soil Conservation Service, the experience was technical—we built dams, dikes, levees, and irrigation. When I was with the Forest Service, I was mainly concerned with road building. After ten years as an engineering tech, I figured out that getting an engineering degree was the only way I'd be able to do what I really wanted to do. I was working in western North Dakota with the Forest Service in 1985 when DU started their new habitat office out there. They were staffing up, so I began as a technician with them before working into a regional biologist position."

It's a move he has not regretted. "The thing I like most about the switch is that I don't do anything that is destructive.

Everything I do is very positive; I am always making something better, either enhancing or creating. I have not done a
project with DU that has given me any remorse or regrets
whatever about what I was doing to the environment. I feel
fortunate about that, because I don't think a lot of engineers
have that same opportunity. It's great!"

McDonough estimates that he spends 50 percent of his
time outdoors and 50 percent indoors. "We're able to break it
up fairly well, too," he adds. "It isn't like I'm in the office for a
month and then out for a month. Several days a week really
make it a nice mix."

Although McDonough works mainly with the biologist
on the team, he also works with state and federal managers.
On occasion he even finds it necessary to address a group.
"Public-speaking ability is a very important attribute in my
job. I also do a lot of letter and report writing. Proper paperwork to support our projects is necessary to obtain permits."

Unfortunately, jobs like his are few. McDonough offers
some advice for those who find his job attractive. "The perfect
engineer for wildlife in general would be a combination of civil
and environmental. Combining the civil engineer's training in
soils and foundations, which would allow him to build or create
an outdoor habitat, with an environmental engineer's expertise
in water treatment and water quality would give a new graduate
an unlimited ability in working with wildlife.

"I wish there were a lot of job openings," he adds. "More
habitats and resources are needed but funds are not available.
You may need to take a job that you're not totally enamored
with but that will give you good experience to add to your résumé
for the time when you find the job you've always wanted. And
you might start as a technician, as I did, and work into higher-
level jobs as they become available."

See Civil Engineering, page 113.

Environmental Engineer
Kathleen Schaefer

Kathleen Schaefer says that her choice of environmental engineering came by fluke, not by design. "When I went to college I decided to major in engineering on a whim," she explains. "Fortunately, my high school counselor hadn't let me drop math and science so I had the technical background to get into engineering."

Schaefer initially took her bachelor's in civil engineering into a job in facilities engineering but changed to environmental engineering because there was more demand in that field. She is now working toward a master's degree in chemical engineering.

Schaefer is a water resources engineer with the Fairfax, Virginia, engineering consulting firm of Dewberry and Davis. "My basic concern is with clean water," she says. "If it is not clean I will see that it is cleaned after industrial use."

Use of the computer, especially for modeling water systems, is very important on Schaefer's job. "Computers have given us capabilities to solve problems that were too difficult to solve in the past when we followed rules of thumb and tables. With the computer we can model the specific water system, define the migration of pollutants much better, and make much closer calculations."

Schaefer likes the variety her job provides. Although each day is different, a sample day could begin by meeting with a client to discuss a problem with a water system. Then she would model the system on the computer, analyze the situation from the model, and write a report. She would also call the appropriate regulatory agency to confirm the pertinent regulations.

Although she doesn't get outside as much as she would like—"I now go out about two days a month, but it goes in spurts from a solid week out to three months without any outdoor work"—being outdoors is another aspect of environmental engineering that Schaefer really likes. She also enjoys client interaction. On the down side she says that big, time-consuming projects begin to get old after a while.

Schaefer cites math and science as key background courses for environmental engineering. Enjoying the outdoors is also important. Computer knowledge is essential, but Schaefer says that the models and tools are changing rapidly and can be learned on each job. She advises learning a computer language and gaining basic familiarity with computers rather than intensive study.

Although Schaefer says career paths for environmental engineers are quite varied, a typical pattern begins with the engineer working on some aspect of design for seven to ten years and then becoming a project manager who supervises three to five engineers. The next step up is department manager, with supervisory responsibility for ten to thirty engineers. Becoming principal of a firm is the final step.

"One of the bad things about engineering," she confides candidly, "is that although engineers make more money initially than people in many other careers, the pay levels off rapidly."

One project she remembers with pleasure involved work on a site adjacent to Puget Sound in Seattle with a wood-treating plant whose chemicals had seeped into the groundwater system. The client was willing to clean up the area but lacked money for the immediate massive cleanup mandated by the regulatory agencies. "This project took two engineers two years to work on," she remembers. "The situation was made more difficult because of the tide fluctuation, and I spent a lot of time in the field. We had a wonderful client for whom I had a lot of empathy."

"The ability to write is very important on my job," says Schaefer. "I write proposals and reports—guidance on doing the job and a summary of the work that has been done. The wording can be very important." Schaefer admits that she had to study on her own to improve her writing.

She also suggests that a broad background is especially helpful in this field. "I would encourage environmental engineers to take more liberal arts courses because they need to understand sociology and philosophy as well as technical matters."

Schaefer cites no one specific personality trait that environmental engineers should have but points out that all engineers need to be inquisitive about how things work and enjoy solving problems. She adds, "The field is so diverse that one can find his or her own niche, no matter what it is."

See Environmental Engineering, page 114.

Geotechnical Engineer
Art O'Brien

"You have to like to get your hands dirty to be a geotechnical engineer," declares Art O'Brien, "because when you're out gathering samples you will get dirty. And you're out in all kinds of weather and all seasons."

Hands-on work was not the only thing that attracted Art O'Brien to his career. "My enjoyment of the outdoors was a part of the reason for choosing geotechnical engineering," this soft-spoken engineer admits quickly. "Initially I went into civil engineering to use my math and science interests. Geotechnical engineering, a branch of civil engineering, interested me because there's a lot of judgment involved. I also liked the fact that we take projects from the very beginning to the very end."

O'Brien has a bachelor's degree in civil engineering and a master's in civil engineering with a geotechnical engineering specialty. He is currently the department manager for the Solid Waste Engineering Group at CH2M Hill in Hernden, Virginia. His fondness for geotechnical engineering is evident as he speaks about the career.

Some of the skills needed for this career aren't necessarily learned in school, O'Brien points out. "Writing can be learned on the job or in writing courses after graduation. People management skills are also needed. Encouraging and motivating people—not only peers and people working in the company, but also subcontractors outside the company—are important.

"One of the difficult things about geotechnical engineering," he admits, "is that the natural materials you're dealing with—properties deposited by Mother Nature—are often highly variable. Oftentimes your testing isn't necessarily representative, so you have to be alert for changes. That can be frustrating." Major changes don't often need to be done, he adds, but small changes requiring quick adjustments do. "But if you're out there you can usually make those changes quickly and they don't affect the progress of the project."

O'Brien indicates that new graduates with a master's degree usually start out as staff engineers. "They do field observations. As the career progresses, less time is spent outside and more time managing and planning. The next level is project engineer, and then project manager. The project management role means more time spent as a team leader working with the client and guiding and managing the project and staff engineers who are gathering information and doing analyses. A next step may be starting your own business."

About his current management position, O'Brien says, "I have taken my geotechnical engineering experience and related it to the solid waste side of geotechnical engineering. So I've expanded my geotechnical engineering into a much broader perspective.

"That means," he adds regretfully, "that I don't get out as much as I used to." He's not sorry he made this move, however. "In my current position I have to keep lots of balls in the air and don't have the opportunity to focus on one specific task or item. At times it is frustrating. It would be nice to be able to do one thing and follow it all the way through again. Now I have to rely on others to do that.

"The learning process starts as you get out of school, and one of the things I enjoy greatly about moving up is the opportunity to train the younger engineers right out of school. So although I'm not out in the field as much as I used to be, I am teaching and sharing my experiences with people who are out in the field."

O'Brien advises persons interested in this career to "develop strong math, science, and problem-solving skills. You will need problem-solving skills throughout an entire engineering career, whatever field of engineering you may be in. An extremely inquisitive mind is also vital to performing adequately in this field."

See Geotechnical Engineering, page 116.

*"**I** must go down to the seas again, to the lonely sea
    and the sky,
And all I ask is a tall ship and a star to steer her by;
And the wheel's kick and the wind's song and the white sails
    shaking,
And a gray mist on the sea's face, and a gray dawn breaking."*
John Masefield, "Sea Fever"

Marine Careers

The sea and work on the sea hold a great attraction for many. For some this may mean a career in oceanography (covered in chapter 5) that involves graduate study as well as research. For others it may mean working on ships, as a diver, or in the fishing industry.

Ships offer quite a variety of positions. Many are not in the outdoors, though the deck positions do involve outdoor work. One can work either on a commercial ship that is a part of the U.S. merchant marine or in the U.S. armed services in the Coast Guard or the Navy.

Commercial diving may also involve the sea; although some commercial diving settings are on inland bodies of water, a great many are in the marine environment. The fishing industry and related careers are also covered in this chapter.

Merchant Marine

Salary Range: varies; assistant engineer, $15,600 to $17,800; chief engineer, about $54,000; captain, $28,600 to $31,300; purser, $20,000 to $25,900

Educational Requirements: four-year nautical school degree for officers; appropriate training for specialized

jobs such as cook; for seaman positions, high school
degree is an asset

Employment Outlook: poor to fair

Merchant marine careers cover the multiplicity of tasks needed to
keep a ship going. They fall into four basic divisions. The deck group
is in charge of the navigation and handling of the ship; the engine
group keeps the ship in operation, which includes making any necessary repairs; the purser group handles business and accounting;
and the steward group takes care of meals and living quarters.

Life on board ship is quite different from any other type of
work. It is confining because staffers can leave the ship only when
they are off duty and the ship is in port. Because of cargo loading or
unloading duties, it may be difficult to get leave.

Older and smaller ships have more-limited living areas, which
might mean sharing rooms and bathrooms, and less-spacious
recreation facilities. Private rooms, air conditioning, and television
are standard features of new ships, however.

The length of voyages varies considerably from several weeks
to many months, depending on whether the ship travels internationally or on the inland waterways of the United States. Basically, however, deck officers and sailors spend most of their time away from
their homes and families.

A high school diploma is not needed for lower-level seaman
jobs, but high school graduates will have an edge in getting positions and moving up within the ranks. Engineers and deck officers
must have graduated from accredited nautical schools, most of
which offer four-year programs.

The outlook for this career is very limited. New technology
and new automated equipment mean that fewer workers are
needed. Competition for jobs opened when staff members leave is
quite keen.

Licensing and documentation of all merchant mariners in the
United States is done by the U.S. Coast Guard. Persons seeking
seafaring employment should contact the nearest U.S. Coast
Guard Regional Examination Center to obtain local advice and
regulation explanations.

Deck Group

The captain, sometimes called a master, is the highest-ranking officer on the ship. As such, he or she is responsible for the ship, all workers on the ship, and all operations of the ship. A captain is the administrator who oversees all work, represents the shipowner, and also does some navigating as a check on the work of the ship's officers. This immensely responsible position includes making decisions about saving a ship in trouble at sea, ordering supplies and services for the ship, and ensuring all aspects of safe working conditions for the crew. In port the captain must clear the vessel through customs and may need to contact the American consulate or discuss business with agents of the owner in foreign ports.

Chief mates are in charge of the other deck officers as well as overseeing the loading and unloading of cargo. Each mate is assigned a four-hour watch, during which he or she navigates the ship. During this time, the mate follows the captain's orders as to speed and course. Chief mates also record the ship's position at given times, post lookouts, and make records of their watches in the ship's log. If anything unusual happens, they must tell the captain immediately.

Second mates have special duties with regard to navigation. They not only check the instruments every day and keep the navigation charts updated, but they also maintain and repair navigation equipment. Like chief mates, each second mate is assigned a four-hour watch.

The lowest-ranking deck officers are the third mates, usually licensed officers with the least experience. They assist the chief mate in supervising cargo loading and unloading, ensure that the lifeboats and other lifesaving equipment are ready for emergency use, and figure the ship's position.

Although deck officers live and work in comfortable quarters with their own rooms or cabins, working outdoors means that they experience all types of weather on board ship, from tropical heat to subfreezing cold, as well as storms at sea. They also spend weeks or months at a time away from home.

Deck officers must successfully pass examinations to work at all levels. These examinations draw upon their experience as they work up from third to first mate. Third mate applicants must either have had three years' minimum experience at sea or have graduated from an approved maritime school. These four-year programs give a solid grounding in the skills needed to handle a ship and include other related courses, such as construction, engineering, and law, as well as liberal arts.

The entry-level deck job is the ordinary seaman—an unskilled worker who does general maintenance work. The next step up is the able seaman, who takes two-hour turns at steering the ship, does general upkeep work, handles deck equipment and all gear, and practices fire prevention and fire-fighting methods.

Able seamen with experience can advance to the position of quartermaster, which involves navigation and being in charge of the ship while it is in port. The highest-ranking seamen are the boatswains; they take orders directly from the ship's officers and supervise the other deck seamen.

Engine Group

The engine group, which operates and maintains the engines and other ship machinery, is presided over by the chief engineers. They oversee the engine area, including the boiler room and the electrical, refrigeration, and heating systems, in addition to sanitary systems and water supplies. Repairs, replacement of parts, and fire prevention and control are also part of their job.

The next level down in the engineering department consists of the first assistant engineers. They supervise the crew in tasks such as starting, stopping, and controlling the speed of the main engines, and they repair and maintain the engines and other ship machinery. Below them are the second assistant engineers, who monitor the water levels, steam pressure, and oil and water temperatures in the boilers, condensers, and evaporators. Next are the third assistant engineers, who supervise the engine room operation.

Other engine-related tasks are performed by oilers, who keep moving parts of engines and equipment greased and lubricated; firemen-watertenders, who ensure that the steam pressure remains constant; wipers, who clean machinery and boilers; electricians, who maintain and repair electrical equipment; and refrigeration engineers, who maintain refrigeration equipment for perishable cargoes.

Unlike deck workers, who experience all kinds of weather on deck, the engine room workers work indoors around hot engines and equipment.

Purser Group

The purser group handles paperwork such as payroll, tariffs, customs, and payment for supplies. Clerical work for other departments of the ship may also be handled by pursers. On smaller ships this work is handled by the captain.

Steward Group

The steward group is responsible for preparing and serving meals and maintaining the living quarters. The chief steward, who plans meals and orders food, supervises the other staff, which includes chief cook, baker, and mess staff.

Fishing

Salary Range: average is $17,200

Educational Requirements: none; skills are learned on the job, although courses in boat navigation, handling, and safety and engine and radio maintenance are helpful

Employment Outlook: poor

The fishing industry is located along the seacoasts of the country. Fishers may work close to shore or may go out quite far, depending on the type of fish they pursue. They may work in small boats or on large, modern, commercial fishing ships.

Fishers who fish in bays or harbors or who go out in the morning and return by evening usually fish alone and in small boats not longer than sixty feet. They sometimes use hooks and lines to fish. Some may dig for clams and oysters in the sand in bays or use traps to catch crabs and lobsters.

Offshore or deep-sea fishing takes place 5 to 150 miles from the shore. The ships are usually sixty to two hundred feet long and equipped with refrigerated holds to keep the catch fresh until they return to shore. The fishers trap schools of fish in nets and scoop the trapped fish into the hold. Large ships may remain at sea for many weeks, traveling to find good fishing grounds.

To be in business as a fisher requires a high initial outlay for the purchase of a boat and equipment. The outlook for fishers is not good. Because of overfishing by ships of many nations, the harvest has decreased. The high cost of getting into and staying in business has forced some people out and discouraged others from entering. And although the demand for fish is increasing, a lot of it is being filled by the commercial fisheries industry.

The work is hard, entailing much lifting of heavy fish and equipment. Working and living quarters at sea are usually cramped. Fishers also face the hazard of bad weather at sea. Nowadays, however, with good radios and modern navigational equipment, fishing is not as dangerous as it once was.

Commercial Fisheries

Salary Range: varies depending on educational requirements and size of company
Educational Requirements: vary from none to master's degree or doctorate
Employment Outlook: good

In recent years, commercial fisheries in the United States have grown rapidly as the demand for fisheries products has increased. Expansion is likely to continue in the future, for the market does not appear to be changing. Fisheries also are valued for the recreation they provide. Sport fishing is the second most popular outdoor activity after swimming.

Fisheries face many problems today. Water use—dredging, dam building, or withdrawal for industrial or agricultural purposes—can change the water habitat, either killing fish or interfering with reproduction. Water pollution and overfishing pose grave threats to many fisheries.

Fisheries provide challenging and varied careers, with many options to pursue. Some possible positions are research biologist, manager, administrator, and aquaculturist.

Each career within the fisheries field has its specific requirements. Some, especially in research areas and educational institutions, require advanced training up to a doctorate. A minimum background for other positions is a bachelor's degree in fisheries science, aquatic ecology, or a closely related field. Recently, a master's degree has been required for some entry-level research and management positions in government and private organizations.

Research

Research biologists who work with fisheries study water organisms and how they interact with their environment. They may examine ways that recreational and commercial activities affect the fishery population and relationships between aquatic resources and humans. Research is a key ingredient for managing fisheries resources.

Research areas include genetics, the study of genes and how they produce similarities and differences among species; limnology, the study of plant and animal life in bodies of fresh water such as lakes and ponds; marine biology, the study of organisms living in the sea; pathology, the study of the origins, nature, causes, and development of disease; and physiology, the study of the proper functioning of animals and plants under different conditions.

Research scientists will need broad training in areas such as biology, ecology, statistics, and mathematics, as well as good communications skills. In-depth research on any of the areas above will require a great deal of specific knowledge and probably graduate study in one of these areas.

The major employers of fisheries biologists in the United States and Canada are federal and state or provincial fish and wildlife agencies. International job opportunities, particularly in developing nations, can be found through agencies such as the Peace Corps or the United Nations Food and Agricultural Organization. Other employment opportunities can be found with universities, power companies, the fisheries industry, environmental consulting firms, and nonprofit organizations.

Fisheries Management

Fisheries managers use the results obtained from research in working to improve and change the various aspects of a fishery. For example, they may wish to use the study of genetics and physiology to increase the numbers or size of the fish that are harvested. Managers organize and implement fish-stocking programs, as well as enforce regulations pertaining to fishing or harvest and access by fishermen. They may interview fishers to gather data helpful in the development of fisheries. Public relations is also an important part of fisheries management.

An area of study that is helpful to fisheries managers is biology; in addition, persons interested in becoming managers should study communications, public policy and administration, and sociology.

Aquaculture

Aquaculturists are the persons in the fisheries industry who have the direct work of producing the fish or shellfish. It is important that they know the physiological, nutritional, and environmental needs of the organism being raised, whether it is catfish, crayfish, trout, salmon, oyster, or shrimp. Most fisheries have fairly high density and are quite susceptible to outbreaks of disease; aquaculturists must be familiar with the diseases and health problems of the species being raised.

An aquaculturist's background should include biology and specific study of fish, including nutrition and health. Also important are a knowledge of water chemistry, genetics, and business operations, and an understanding of market economics.

See Profile, page 138.

Fisheries Administration

Another important fisheries career is administration. The administrator oversees, plans, and coordinates the work of other persons in fisheries. Developing and writing laws, regulations, and policies may be done by administrators. The administrator's work in coordinating objectives, preparing budgets, and supervising staff helps in developing priorities among the many research and management activities. The administrator needs to understand the overall relationship between the fishery, the government agency responsible for fisheries, and the public.

These senior-level management positions, which may be in

state or federal government or with private organizations, are held by persons with a great deal of experience in the field. Managing and research often provide good background experience for senior administrators.

Commercial Diving

Salary Range: starting between $18,700 and $26,000; with five years of experience, may increase to $52,000
Educational Requirements: special training courses, many of which are thirty-four weeks in length
Employment Outlook: excellent

Commercial divers work underwater for profit. Divers specialize in the areas of underwater welding, emergency medical care, inspection of underwater work, and nondestructive testing. They work in construction, salvage, or repair, or with offshore oil. This type of work demands a high level of skill and great physical strength. The tasks and settings are varied and challenging.

Some divers specialize in underwater wet welding. Special training is required to learn the techniques of underwater burning and the technology of wet shielded arc welding.

Other divers perform underwater inspection and nondestructive testing. They may clean underwater steel structures, look for and weld defects in steel and concrete structures, and do underwater survey. Training includes underwater photography, preparing technical inspection reports, and using ultrasonic and magnetic particle inspection equipment.

Treatment of injuries and diseases related to diving is the focus of diver medical technicians. Always on hand during diving operations, the emergency medical diver must know how to respond to a variety of medical emergencies and be able to stabilize the patient's condition until better-trained medical authorities can arrive.

Among the varied settings where commercial divers work, oil-field work is expanding and requires a great deal of skill. In oil-field work, divers are used in exploring, drilling, and producing and shipping the oil. Divers working in marine construction do almost any type of underwater work, such as inspecting and repairing breakwaters, pipelines, floating drydocks, bridge foundations, piers, and marine ways.

Salvage work demands many underwater skills, such as the use of underwater metal-cutting equipment and pneumatic, power velocity, and hydraulic tools. It also requires knowledge about ships, cargoes, and how cargoes are loaded. Diving work on dams offers many jobs and requires more skills than most other underwater work; divers do surveying, inspection, some of the actual construction, and some repair work on all types of dams. The last major type of setting for commercial divers is inland work in locations such as rivers, harbors, lakes, and ponds that are part of power systems.

Because the work is very strenuous and the setting quite alien (cold water, waves, darkness, currents, and pressure), a diver must be strong, in excellent physical and mental condition, and able to take the strain this setting presents.

Commercial diving courses take about thirty-four weeks. A high school diploma (or educational and background experience equivalent to that of a high school graduate) is a prerequisite for admission. Essential for the career is the ability to follow written instructions, make calculations, understand and follow blueprint instructions, and write intelligent reports of what was found and what is recommended. A commercial diver must have technological background, electric and electronic experience, engineering training, and organizational ability.

Because commercial diving involves underwater mechanics, the diver must have a high ability in many mechanical fields. For divers to perform their work, they must be able to use cutting and welding equipment and to adapt above-water tools and fittings to underwater jobs, and they must also understand hydraulics and compressed air and be able to adapt these power sources to underwater tasks.

This field, already expanding before the Iraqi devastation of Kuwait, offers great potential for expansion in the 1990s—that man-made disaster has opened up a demand for commercial divers experienced in repair work. Additionally, the awareness of an overdependence on foreign oil has begun a push for more domestic oil supplies, and the U.S. government has begun to subsidize deeper oil drilling. Aging structures also require more inspection and maintenance. As technologies applied to underwater work have developed, such as the ability to work at deeper levels for longer periods of time, more jobs have opened up.

Commercial divers do not work full-time. Depending on their jobs, they work about 60 percent of the time, or about 160 days a year. For steady employment the diver must travel, following his or her employer, or search for a new job when one is completed.

See Profile, page 141.

Resources

Commercial Diving

Commercial Diving: Learn to Dive and other pamphlets on specific courses, College of Oceaneering, Los Angeles Harbor, 272 South Fries Avenue, Wilmington, CA 90744-6399 (800-824-9027).

Fisheries

Fisheries as a Profession, American Fisheries Society, 5410 Grosvenor Lane, Suite 110, Bethesda, MD 20814-2199.

Merchant Marine

Information Concerning Employment and Training in the U.S. Merchant Marine (pamphlet), U.S. Department of Transportation, Maritime Administration, Central Region Director, ITM Building, #2 Canal Street, New Orleans, LA 70130-1580 (504-589-6556).

Aquaculturist
Connie Young-Dubovsky

"Aquaculture is a new industry—it's exciting to be in on something new," says Connie Young-Dubovsky eagerly. "People in this field are very enthusiastic and see lots of possibilities. I'm in on the cutting edge—people don't say, 'This is the way it's always been done.'"

Young-Dubovsky is an aquaculture agent with the North Carolina Cooperative Extension Service. Previously she worked as a fish hatchery superintendent at a North Carolina state fish hatchery and as a research assistant at Mississippi State University.

At Mississippi State she worked as a "right-hand woman," running all the research projects, including a USDA-funded grant to study the feasibility of raising the hybrid striped bass in Mississippi as a breed to supplement the catfish industry. She also worked with the well-established catfish industry, trying to produce a bigger fish in a shorter amount of time. She gathered data, analyzed statistics, and wrote reports of the results. In the process, she says, "I got to handle a lot of fish in both outdoor ponds and indoor tanks."

As a fish hatchery superintendent, Young-Dubovsky was responsible for producing striped and hybrid striped bass, largemouth bass, channel catfish, and various species of sunfish for stocking state waterways and impoundments. The experience gave her a chance to apply research to a practical, hands-on situation. The job was a good transition into extension work, which bridges the theoretical and the practical.

Although Young-Dubovsky has enjoyed all of her jobs, she is most enthusiastic about the educational aspect of extension work. "Before I obtained this position I had been working on a teaching certificate because I'm very interested in conservation education," she explains. "Part of being an aquaculture extension agent involves working with conservation education. I give information on the telephone and work on educational programs for schools and local groups.

"Aquaculture is not just fish hatcheries, as many people think. It really is agriculture—farming fish—and as such it is increasingly coming under the jurisdiction of the U.S. Department of Agriculture."

Young-Dubovsky got into fisheries by the process of elimination. When she obtained her bachelor's degree in animal science she intended to enter veterinary school. When she wasn't accepted at a veterinary school, she pursued her interest in fish and obtained a master's degree in fisheries and wildlife.

Her educational background is essential for the work she's doing, she explains. "In my position I need a master's." One can take different routes to work in fisheries, however. Some other options are agricultural engineering, agricultural economics—"an important field as the industry expands"—and biology. She chose her particular path because of her interest in biology.

Young-Dubovsky says there is no such thing as a typical day in her present position. On a recent day she visited some entrepreneurial fish farmers who have been raising catfish and another farmer who recently began stocking trout in a flow-through pond. Their fish had been dying for unknown reasons, so she took some samples of both trout and catfish to a pathology lab.

She spends a lot of time visiting and assisting local fish farmers. "I helped a local farmer, who wanted to raise crawfish, by testing his farm pond water. I also recently helped a catfish farmer examine the possibilities for restocking his farm.

"Many of the problems I deal with relate to a fish-kill, the water quality, or helping farmers learn about the possibilities for changing their programs. Disease is a real problem in aquaculture. I'm not a disease specialist, but I take specimens to the lab, where vets trained in fish pathology will take over."

Young-Dubovsky also spends a lot of time in her office answering questions by telephone and obtaining necessary information. "An important personality trait for my position is being a people person—you need to like interacting with

people," she says. "Because there are very few women in these positions I have to make more of an effort to establish my credibility."

One negative she has encountered is that her jobs, especially the hatchery position, have involved extra hours. "The state fish hatchery position was very intensive, not an eight-to-five job," she says. "I need more diversity in my life with time off for myself.

"One piece of advice I can give anyone interested in this career is to get as much experience as possible. Even if you volunteer or work for room and board, experience is more valuable than anything else—you need to get your feet wet. Because contacts are important, you should also attend professional meetings and meet people in the field."

See Aquaculture, page 134.

Commercial Diver
Tom Mosher

Tom Mosher has a love-hate relationship with his career. "I love diving," he says emphatically, "but I hate the politics of the diving industry.

"I like being underwater and doing the challenging things we do underwater," he elaborates. "We are expected to accomplish tasks the average person wouldn't do." Yet he dislikes the politics involved in getting jobs, and he's seen persons fired from jobs with no reason given. "Luck—being available when someone is needed—plays a greater role in finding diving jobs than your skills."

Work sites for divers can be inland or offshore. Inland divers work in rivers, lakes, sewers, and power plants, and on dams. For example, intakes made of concrete and steel supply water from a river or lake for industrial water uses and have filters that need to be inspected, repaired, and replaced continually. Offshore divers work in the ocean "from the beach out"—much of the work involves exploration for and production of oil and gas. Work for offshore divers is more varied as well as more dangerous than that of inshore divers.

Divers receive hourly wages plus additional pay for penetration and depth dives. On penetration dives—when they enter a confined space such as a pipeline and can't surface immediately—they are paid by the horizontal foot. For depth work the extra pay is by the vertical foot. "With depth pay you can earn close to $1,000 a day on a 950-foot dive," Mosher says. This extra pay helps to compensate for the added danger and the time divers must take to decompress from depth dives. For example, in saturation dives every hundred feet require a day to decompress. "Ten days in the decompression chamber can be pretty boring," Mosher says matter-of-factly.

Mosher doesn't talk a great deal about danger, but he does say that in a recent six-month job he was almost killed three times and got the bends three times. (*Bends* is a nickname for decompression sickness, which occurs when a diver exceeds his time limit at a specified depth.)

Mosher has worked both inland and offshore: "I prefer diving offshore but I don't like the lifestyle as much—it is much harder to stay healthy. Offshore we work very irregular hours. We never know when we will dive. Inland we work more regular hours."

Because of the skills required and dangers involved in offshore work, divers serve an apprenticeship as "tenders" for two to four years before being allowed to work offshore as divers. A tender essentially takes care of the divers, tending the hose while they are underwater and carrying supplies while they are in the decompression chamber. They also do dirty work such as deck cleanup. Mosher says tenders generally are not treated well and earn from $5 to $9 an hour compared with the $10 to $17 hourly rates divers receive. Tenders do some diving, depending on their skill level, and it is their skill that determines when they "break out" as divers.

According to Mosher, ideal candidates for diving positions are twenty-two years old, single, and have a construction background and mechanical aptitude. "You travel a lot in commercial diving to find jobs, and you don't have a guaranteed income," he explains. "At the beginning you can be very poor. This kind of life wreaks havoc on building or keeping relationships. The divorce rate in the diving industry is extremely high. If you don't want a family or a settled life, then this kind of life is fine."

Mosher believes one of the most important traits commercial divers need is something that can't be taught—common sense. "Divers need to be able to look at things, see what needs to be done, and do it," he explains. "A few commercial divers haven't been to dive school. If I were to do it again I would consider the option of finding the least expensive school that would give an air certificate." (An air certificate allows a diver to work using tanks containing only oxygen, at depths to about 190 feet; for dives over 190 feet, a diver must have another certificate allowing him to use mixed gases.)

Mosher hasn't met many women divers. "Diving has its good moments, but it is cold, dirty, and hard work," he explains. "You will get dirtier than you ever believed you would get. It's a very hard lifestyle—physically and emotionally demanding. You may deal with the whole range of emotions in one day—from fear to exhilaration—and it can be emotionally exhausting. We get up at odd hours and deal with miseries from being very cold to very hot. It's not a lifestyle most women would be a part of."

"As long as man is working near or on the water there will always be a need for divers," Mosher states. He adds: "Diving is hard, dangerous, dirty work, and your chances of succeeding as a professional diver are slim because it's definitely not a career for everyone. You should not get into diving for the money, but because you love working on or in the water."

See Commercial Diving, page 135.

"If all the year were playing holidays,
To sport would be as tedious as to work."
William Shakespeare, *King Henry IV*

Recreation

As the American work force has gained increased leisure time, it has invested more time in organized recreation. This has meant more jobs for recreation workers, who are involved in planning, organizing, and directing these leisure activities. Outdoor employment for recreation workers is available in sports, camping, hunting, fishing, and nature-oriented activities.

The types of employers vary widely. More than half of all recreation workers are employed by the government, primarily at the municipal and county levels, although others also work in state park systems and for some federal programs. Many work in membership organizations, including the YWCA, the Girl Scouts, and the Red Cross. Many others find employment in social-service organizations, such as senior centers, or residential care facilities, such as group homes and halfway houses. Other employers are as varied as wilderness and survival organizations, sports and entertainment centers, camps, travel agencies or companies specializing in vacation trips, hotels and resorts, and apartment complexes.

Settings for recreation programs may be as widely divergent as pristine wilderness areas, city parks, health clubs, and cruise ships. While there are some exceptions, jobs generally follow the population, and the majority of the jobs are in urban or suburban areas or in camps in states with higher populations.

Many recreation positions are full-time, but there is a very strong component of part-time or weekend work and a hefty increase of workers in the summertime. There are also many volunteers. In the field of recreation, part-time and volunteer work often lead to full-time positions.

It is often possible to find satisfactory full-time employment in outdoor recreation by combining several careers. For example, a high school environment teacher might spend the summer teaching wilderness survival skills. A ski patroller may work in the off-season on ski trails or ski lift maintenance and construction. It is even possible to combine writing and tourboat guiding, as the profile of Tim Jones in this chapter demonstrates. Because of the variety of positions in recreation, it is possible to creatively combine several to suit the worker's preferred lifestyle.

Because the careers are so diverse, educational requirements vary widely. Many summer positions don't even require a high school diploma, while many administrative positions require graduate education. College graduates with majors in recreation, leisure studies, or parks fill many career positions, but the private sector may settle for a bachelor's degree and aptitude or experience. Specialized skills and certificates are required for many jobs, such as diving or lifesaving.

Camping Careers

Salary Range: varies depending on size of camp and position; a director in a small camp may earn $24,000 to $26,500, while a director in a larger camp might earn $30,000 to $40,000

Educational Requirements: usually a bachelor's degree, and often graduate work for career camping positions

Employment Outlook: good; with the move to specialty camps such as equestrian or tennis, more opportunities are opening

Camps differ tremendously in size and focus; this determines the types of positions each camp will have available. Generally all positions except some in administration are seasonal, although this depends on the focus of the camp. There is currently a trend toward more positions that have full-time outdoor responsibilities.

Camping positions call for a great variety of backgrounds and disciplines. They use the principles of social work, psychology, physical education, recreation, and education, while also calling for skills in business management, nutrition and food service, and repair and maintenance of buildings.

Career positions in camping include camp administrator, who is in charge of several camp programs; camp director, who is in charge of the administration and program of a specific camp; associate director, who assists the administrator and often directs the camp program; outdoor program director, who coordinates, plans, and administers a specific outdoor program; and trip leader (title varies), who leads groups on extended outdoor experiences.

The camp administrator is usually located in a metropolitan area and just visits the camps, but the director usually stays on a resident camp site year-round.

Cruise Ship Positions

Salary Range: varies tremendously depending on the specific job, required background, and ship size

Educational Requirements: depend on the specific jobs performed

Employment Outlook: appears to be good with new, larger, resort-type ships entering the field; jobs should remain very competitive.

Cruise ships can be exciting places to work, because they present the opportunity to travel to different places, but staff and crew members often have little time to go ashore. Cruise ships offer a variety of jobs, few of which match exactly the positions shown on the popular television show "The Love Boat." In fact, persons interested in cruise ship jobs should be aware that such jobs are not easy. The work is usually hard, the hours long, and the positions difficult to obtain.

The work focuses on the safety and happiness of the passengers, and all persons working on board who have any contact with the passengers are expected to keep this in mind. Friendliness and the ability to get along well with others are important assets in cruise ship positions.

Jobs fall into two categories: staff and crew. Staff members include the cruise director and cruise staff, who are responsible for ship activities and excursions onshore; entertainers, such as musicians, singers, dancers, magicians, and comedians; and sometimes lecturers, fitness and recreational specialists, or persons who handle children's activities or arts and crafts. In general, staff members have more contact with the passengers than crew members do.

Numbered among the crew workers are the cabin stewards, who keep the cabins clean; the deck stewards, who clean and serve food; and the bar stewards, who serve drinks. Waiters and busboys clean the dining areas and serve food, and the kitchen crew prepares the food. Hairdressers and boutique and casino operators may also be part of the crew.

All workers on cruise ships work seven days a week; vacation time varies depending on the specific job. The staff positions have fairly high burnout rates; typically staffers spend about three years in these positions. Those who stay longer can work their way into cruise director careers.

Being able to speak a number of languages is an asset for cruise ship staff. A good knowledge of recreational activities and fitness is important, as is the ability to live in a situation with little privacy. Ability to work on a moving ship, especially when the seas are rough, is essential.

Because of job competition, the best strategy is to either work through agencies that recruit entertainment staff for cruise ships or contact the cruise lines directly.

Staff

The cruise director oversees all shipboard activities (entertainment, fitness, hairdresser, boutiques, and casinos) and onshore excursions. Duties include supervision of staffers who organize walks, aerobics, contests, and movies, as well as the lecturers. Onshore excursions involve many more details to deal with and problems to solve, including checking to make sure that port services still meet expectations. Working hours usually begin at 7 A.M. and may continue to 1 A.M. with some time off during the day.

Entertainers perform a certain number of shows per cruise; on smaller ships they may be involved with other shipboard or on-shore activities.

Crew

Cabin stewards keep cabins clean and supplied in addition to serving food and drinks to passengers in cabins. They are able to go on-shore on a rotating basis but often spend free time sleeping. These employees begin work at about 6 A.M. and end at 10 P.M., with some time off during the day.

Waiters must be able to tell passengers the ingredients of the items on the menu, take the orders, and serve the food. They must be sensitive to passenger tastes and substitute another dish if what is served is not satisfactory.

The main responsibilities of busboys are clearing the tables and refilling water glasses and coffee cups. They also assist waiters in bringing food out of the kitchen. A waiter may serve about five tables, and a busboy ten. Hours for both waiters and busboys are usually from 6 A.M. to 10 A.M., 11 A.M. to 3 P.M., and 5:30 P.M. to 10 P.M. Another shift, from 11 P.M. to 1:30 A.M., is generally rotated among workers. There is very little time off.

Bar stewards take orders for drinks and serve them, which gives the stewards plenty of time to interact with passengers. They usually work one of two shifts: 9 A.M. to 5 P.M., or 4 P.M. to 1 or 2 A.M.

Diving Instruction

Salary Range: depends on position; full-time instructors at retail facilities start at about $15,000 and can earn as much as $40,000 to $50,000; owners of stores or resorts make more

Educational Requirements: certification to teach

Employment Outlook: excellent

Another recreational pursuit that provides opportunities for outdoor careers is scuba diving. Because of the danger of underwater diving, recreational scuba divers must be certified to dive. This certification comes from organizations such as the Professional Association of Diving Instructors (PADI), the National Association of Underwater Instructors (NAUI), the YMCA, and Scuba Schools International, which have courses in diving and require diving instructors.

Diving instruction offers opportunities to travel and to work in unusual locations. Basically, dive instructors teach the skills of diving to their students. They also work to ensure that their students remain interested in and active in the sport through additional dive travel experiences.

Underwater swimming and diving skills are the basic essentials for this career, and all who begin instruction courses must be certified to dive. Instructors must also be certified in dive instruction, which involves taking instructors' courses and passing an examination for the certification. Rescue courses are required. Other courses give specific instruction in teaching diving. Diving instructors can also take courses qualifying them to teach some of the popular specialties, such as wreck diving, deep diving, underwater photography, underwater navigating, search-and-recovery diving, and night diving.

PADI has developed a dive instruction course that has been recognized by the American Council on Education for college and university credit. PADI instructors are also recognized worldwide; the association's dive centers are located in more than fifty countries.

As a recreational sport, scuba diving is increasing in popularity. Previously remote areas of the world are being opened up. More people are considering diving a fun, relaxing recreation. Consequently, the demand for qualified dive instructors is expected to increase in the 1990s. Many diving instructors work full-time through dive shops, and some teach on a part-time basis.

The Horse Industry

Salary Range: varies; grooms from $7,800 to $13,200; riding instructors about $25 per hour; trainers between $14,200 and $16,200 to start

Educational Requirements: vary depending on the job; most entry-level positions provide on-the-job training

Employment Outlook: good because of the growth in recreational riding

Quite a variety of careers relate to the horse industry. The level of education required ranges from a doctorate or a professional degree all the way down to a high school diploma. The level of contact with horses also ranges from daily contact or work in horse shows, rodeos, or the racing industry to infrequent contact in careers that involve issues related to horses.

Examples of careers involving daily contact with horses and a high level of education include veterinarian, geneticist, animal nutritionist, and extension horse or animal specialist. Careers requiring slightly less education include pedigree analyst, county agriculture agent, farm or ranch manager, humane society official, and mounted police officer.

Horse shows, rodeos, and the racing industry offer positions such as horse show manager, judge, course and jump designer, publicist, security person, and photographer. Positions that require a great deal of skill and experience are jockey, trainer, driver, and rodeo rider.

See Profile, page 159.

Outfitting and Guiding Hunts

Salary Range: beginning guides make $500 to $600 a month; experienced hunters earn more, but pay varies widely depending on type of hunt and the difficulty in finding the quarry

Educational Requirements: guide schools teach the basics

Employment Outlook: there will be a continuing demand to replace persons leaving the field

As the lure of hunting and fishing in the wild continues to attract the unskilled across the country, the need for professional hunting guides will continue. Guides are hired by outfitters who are required, in most states, to have a license before they may outfit hunting expeditions. The outfitters handle insurance and equipment and are liable for the actions of guides.

A professional guide takes hunters who have no knowledge of the wilderness and helps them make a kill. Typical game varieties in demand are elk, deer, bears, antelope, and different fishes.

This profession demands a thorough knowledge of the wilderness, especially the ability to track and find animals. Not only do guides help largely unskilled hunters, but they also have to cover a fair amount of territory, usually by foot, and carry heavy loads. In bear hunting, for example, bait must be carried in, and when a shot has been successful, the trophy must be cleaned and carried out.

Guides must be able to outfit the inexperienced hunter with the proper equipment and, if necessary, know how to use pack animals. Expertise with weapons—guns, bow and arrow, or fishing rod—is essential.

Hunting guides must be able to work well with people. Those who hire the services of a guide may be totally unskilled in wilderness lore or shooting a gun and may not even be a pleasant associate. The guide must give each person his or her money's worth and a sense that the hunt was successful, even if they do not come back with a trophy.

In addition to having a knowledge of the woods, guides must know about the habits of animals and how to best locate the particular quarry of the hunt. Fishing guides must know about fishing, as well as river floating. Other important skills are camping and lifesaving.

Hunting guides work quite hard. Hunting season usually encompasses only the months of September through November, although there may be winter hunts. If it is a family owned or operated business, more time may be spent outside, sometimes as much as six months either guiding or scouting to prepare for the upcoming season. The continuing demand for good hunting guides reflects the demand for such services and the high turnover rate among guides because of the time away from home this career requires.

Ski Patrolling

Salary Range: from $5 to $15 an hour, depending upon
   experience and size of the resort
Educational Requirements: winter emergency care
   and first-aid courses
Employment Outlook: good

The main concern of ski patrollers is the safety of the skiing public.
Working at ski areas, they provide first-aid and rescue services for
injured or lost skiers and offer information about skiing safety.

Ski patrollers typically spend about eight hours a day on
the slopes, although they may work longer if there is danger of
avalanches. At the beginning of each work day the patrollers are
given instructions and special work assignments, which might
include helping with ski races scheduled for that day and posting
signs to warn of hazards or give special instructions.

Patrollers also ski the course before it is opened to the public
to look for and smooth out ridges or piles of snow that may
have been left by the huge grooming machines that work on the
ski slopes every night. Signs must be checked for ice or anything
else that makes them difficult to read, and patrollers must make
certain that the ropes that mark the boundary of the ski areas are
visible.

One patroller always stays at the summit headquarters, a duty
that is rotated, to answer the phone and radio. If this person needs
to leave for any reason, he or she will radio for a replacement. All
ski patrollers wear radios for the instant contact that is necessary
in emergencies.

Avalanches are common problems in the western United
States, and avalanche forecasting, which is sometimes done
through the ski resort's own weather station, is important for
patrolling. If avalanche problems are suspected, patrollers go to
the slopes early to defuse the situation by triggering the avalanche
before skiers arrive on the slopes.

Ski patrollers must also be able to evacuate ski lifts in case of emergency: This involves descending the lifts on the cables and lowering skiers by rope to the ground.

This career demands great skill in skiing, including the ability to ski tough terrain. Patrollers must have successfully completed courses in winter emergency procedures and cardiopulmonary resuscitation. Training in handling toboggans, lift evacuation, and other safety procedures is also required. Since ski patrolling is so physically demanding, few persons stay in it for a lifetime.

Ski patrolling is a seasonal job from mid-November to sometime in April. Ski patrollers usually balance this career by working summer seasonal jobs such as construction. Many resorts also use volunteer patrollers to assist their professional patrollers. Although the field reflects the economic situation of the moment, as well as weather conditions, new ski-patrolling positions are available every year because of attrition.

See Profile, page 162.

Skydiving Instruction

Salary Range: varies, depending on place and type of instruction; for accelerated free-fall instruction, fees are about $20 per student

Educational Requirements: training is available through the United States Parachute Association

Employment Outlook: growing

Essentially, a skydiving instructor teaches persons how to jump out of airplanes. All instructors must be experienced sky divers who are able to teach. This industry is not regulated by the federal government, and only a few states have regulations. A majority of sky divers, instructors, and drop zones (mainly airports where the dives take place) belong to the United States Parachute Association (USPA).

A private organization concerned with the safety of the sport, the USPA publishes a magazine with a focus on safety in the sport. Additionally, instructors who teach at USPA drop zones must have taken USPA classes on teaching and pass written, oral, and practical tests. There are three levels of instructors: At the top is the jump-master, followed by the instructor, and then the instructor-examiner.

There are three methods of practical instruction after the student has completed a course. The static line jump is from a height of 3,000 feet, and the student's parachute is activated when he or she leaves the plane. In the tandem jump (also at 3,000 feet), the student is a passenger, attached to the instructor at the shoulders and hips, and the instructor operates the parachute. For accelerated free fall, the jump is from at least 10,000 feet. The student jumps at the same time as the instructors, and they do some maneuvers before the parachute is pulled. For the initial jump and levels 1 to 3, two instructors jump with each student. For levels 4 to 7, one instructor jumps with each student. This method allows for maximum instruction in practice and immediate correction if it is needed.

Skydiving is a growing sport with increasing numbers of students. Pay for instruction generally is not high, although it varies from place to place. Many instructors teach because they enjoy the work and not because of high pay. Professional instructors who work for larger operations may receive higher wages.

Skydiving is a highly seasonal sport. The majority of the drop zones operate only on the weekends in warm weather, although some do operate full-time through the summer. In mild climates where there is a high population and good demand, it is possible to teach skydiving full-time.

The Tourism Industry

Salary Range: varies tremendously; tour escorts make between $225 and $550 a week

Educational Requirements: a high school degree is the minimum; college or training courses by tour companies will aid in finding jobs

Employment Outlook: good

Tour companies employ drivers and tour guides as well as administrators and salespeople. The job with the most potential for outdoor work is that of tour escort or guide.

Tour escorts lead groups of people on trips known as packaged tours that give travelers a complete itinerary with transportation, lodging, and sightseeing all arranged. Other tour guides, called step-on guides, meet buses and take them on one-day trips around a certain area. Occasionally, bus drivers also provide commentary for one-day trips. Most localities have requirements for step-on guides that usually include obtaining a license by passing a test. Many guides say this about their career: "Where else can you get paid for talking all you want and telling people where to go?"

Vicky Schwartz left an office position and MBA degree and has worked for four years as a tour guide in the Washington, D.C., area. She is an independent contractor who works for ten different companies. "As a professional tour guide I wear many hats," she says. "I have had to be a diplomat, a walking encyclopedia, a navigator, a counselor/therapist, a restaurant critic, a real estate specialist, an alcohol/tobacco regulation enforcer, a labor relations specialist . . . and the list goes on.

"I like continuing to learn and build my knowledge, choosing my hours, and being outside. It's also very exciting to be around Capitol Hill, see what is going on about town, and meet prominent lawmakers. Although you can make good money as a tour guide, it is a seasonal job and not one on which to support yourself year-round."

Work for step-on guides is seasonal, while tour escorts who work with packaged tours work year-round. This work can be quite demanding, since it involves working seven days a week for many consecutive weeks, lifting luggage, and trying hard to keep all tour members happy.

Tour guides need excellent verbal communications skills and the ability to interact well with people. They must be able to think on their feet and deal with crises or unexpected changes that may occur, such as bus breakdowns or airline strikes. It's also important that they enjoy learning about an area and communicating that information to tour members.

Degrees in tourism are available at some colleges, and some large tour companies provide training, but most tour escorts learn their skills on the job, often working alongside seasoned escorts to learn about tour destinations and company policies. Some persons arrive at escort and guide positions through contacts gained while working in other segments of the travel industry, such as at a hotel or with an airline. Others obtain jobs by sending résumés to travel companies or tour operators whose destinations attract them.

The outlook for tour escorts and step-on guides is good, although the amount of expansion in the travel industry is directly related to the economy. When the economy is booming, people are willing to spend money on trips and the field expands; the opposite occurs during recessionary times.

See Profile, page 165.

Resources

Camping

Careers in Camping (pamphlet) includes a list of camping organizations. Contact American Camping Association, Bradford Woods, 5000 State Road 67 North, Martinsville, IN 46151-7902 (317-342-8456).

Cruise Ship Work

Employ, which focuses on recreation careers, is available from National Recreation and Park Association, 2775 South Quincy St., Suite 300, Arlington, VA 22206 (703-820-4940). Write for a listing of back issues; each issue costs $5.

Diving Instruction

Four Steps to PADI Open Water Scuba Instructor (pamphlet), PADI, 1251 East Dyer Road, #100, Santa Ana, CA 92705-5605 (714-540-7234).
NAUI Blue Book: A Guide for Leadership Training, NAUI Headquarters, P.O. Box 14650, Montclair, CA 91763-1150 (800-553-6284).

The Horse Industry

Educational Opportunities in the Horse Industry, American Horse Council, 1700 K Street, N.W., #300, Washington, DC 20006.

Outfitters and Guides

A basic directory with a sentence on requirements for outfitters is available from Montana Outfitters & Guides Association, Box 9070, Helena, MT 59601.

Rodeo Riders

Limited information about persons in this career is available from Professional Rodeo Cowboys Association, 101 Pro Rodeo Drive, Colorado Springs, CO 80919-9989 and Women's Professional Rodeo Association, Route 5, Box 698, Blanchard, OK 73010.

Ski Patrolling

Commins, Michael. *Ski Patroller: Can You Make the Grade? Would You Like the Work?* Harrisburg, PA: Stackpole Books, 1990.

Ski Patrol Magazine, which is published quarterly and contains articles about patrolling and various resorts as well as some job listings, is available from National Ski Patrol System, Ski Patrol Building, Suite 100, 133 South Van Gordon, Lakewood, CO 80228 (303-988-1111).

Skydiving Instruction

United States Parachute Association, 1440 Duke Street, Alexandria, VA 22314 (703-836-3495).

Equestrienne
Phyllis Dawson

"The first word I ever said was 'horse.' All I ever wanted to do was ride," says Phyllis Dawson, a riding instructor and three-day event competitor who also trains and boards horses at Windchase Farm near Hillsboro, Virginia.

Although Dawson grew up on a farm and began to teach riding and board horses when she was in high school, she served an apprenticeship to really learn the business. "I was a working student with a top-level competitor," she explains. "In this situation I was totally immersed in the stable and the day-to-day business."

While Dawson says college courses in horsemanship can be a place to start for individuals who have no experience with horses, students do not learn enough from this study to start in the business. "In the horse business experience is very, very, very important," she emphasizes. "Also very important is your reputation for dealing honestly and giving your horses good care."

Dawson begins riding around 8:30 or 9 A.M. each day (although the stable is open earlier); she often starts earlier in the summer to avoid the heat. From 4 P.M. until 7 P.M. she gives riding lessons. "I ride my own high-level competition horses first and then I school the young horses I am training," she explains. "I now have students training with me who do some riding and help with the daily care and mucking stalls. But it has taken a long time to get this reputation.

"Working with horses involves long hours, few days off, low pay, and a lot of hard work. If you really love it, it's a great job—I wouldn't trade it for anything! Some people say to me, 'It must be wonderful to ride horses all day and not have a real job.' They don't understand."

During the event seasons (March to June and the end of August through early November) she enters competitions that test the same horse and rider in different events over three days. The first day is spent on dressage, a series of movements that tests the obedience, suppleness, finesse, and paces of the horse. Dawson compares dressage to the compulsory figures that used to be required in figure-skating competitions. The cross-country course, which is fifteen to eighteen miles long in the upper levels of competition that Dawson rides, is the most important of the events and tests the speed, endurance, boldness, and jumping ability of the horse. The third day of stadium jumping tests the horse's obedience and suppleness, as well as the conditioning that enables it to work the day after the long cross-country competition. The winner of the event is the horse-and-rider pair with the highest cumulative score from all three days.

"If I didn't compete I could take some time off, but competition is what attracts people to train with you," Dawson says. "And to coach you must stay current and in the upper levels of competition. It's all a part of the business." Dawson enjoys coaching, gaining satisfaction from watching her students progress. Additionally, she says that teaching helps her own riding improve.

People who enter this career must really want to do it, Dawson emphasizes. They must be very dedicated, love being outdoors, and love horses and working with them. The career also requires a long-term commitment. "To be in this career you must be able to come back after failures, disappointments, and the loss of a beloved horse. I have heard people say, 'If I don't make it to the top in a year or two I can always change careers.' Let me tell you, you don't make it to the top in a year or two!"

People in the horse business must also be able to relate well to other people, because boarding and training horses as well as teaching riding are all client-based.

Dawson's work goes on in weather extremes from bitter cold to the heat of summer. Even her indoor arena is not heated or air-conditioned. Nevertheless, Dawson says emphatically, "I like almost everything about it! I am totally happy doing what I am doing!" Even winning a lottery would change little about her schedule or work, she says, although she might buy a new truck and wouldn't feel pressured to keep every stall filled.

"There will always be a need for people in horse careers," Dawson declares. "It is a popular sport, so good instructors and trainers will always be in demand. Persons interested in this career must know that you do not get in it for the money. You must do it for the love of horses, of riding, and of training. It would be a terrible career if you didn't really love it."

Dawson's most exciting moment to date has been riding in the 1988 Summer Olympics in Seoul, Korea. To qualify for the U.S. team she went through selection trials in the spring of 1988. At the Olympics she finished tenth in the individual three-day event, making her the highest-placed American. "Riding into that arena and seeing my name in lights with U.S.A. after it was the thrill of a lifetime!"

See The Horse Industry, page 150.

Ski Patroller
Michael Commins

"I spend virtually all my time outdoors—sometimes in the worst weather imaginable," says ski patroller Michael Commins. Commins, a California native, learned to ski as a child, but says he entered this career by chance. "A friend got a job on a ski patrol in Sun Valley [Idaho] and I decided to try it also," he relates. Some eighteen years later he still works in ski patrolling, now as a supervisor at the Grand Targhee Resort in Wyoming.

Ski patrollers promote safe skiing to the public through their contact with skiers and by posting temporary or permanent warning signs. They also give first aid to injured skiers. This includes everything from treating minor injuries to transporting badly injured skiers off the mountain via a toboggan.

"During the day we ski down the slopes about once an hour looking for problems or accidents," Commins explains. "At the end of the day we do the final run, called a *sweep,* to be certain that everyone is off the slopes. We make a visual check and stop often, listening for calls for help and calling out 'Sweep' or 'Final' to warn skiers to get off the slopes."

As ski patrol director, Commins has the additional responsibilities of recruiting, training, and supervising the ski patrollers. He suggests that persons looking for patrolling jobs apply early, because applications often arrive a year in advance.

Commins says that skills required for the job include proficiency in skiing and basic first-aid training. The National Ski Patrol's course in winter emergency care is essential. General outdoor experience in camping and hiking, such as that gained through Boy and Girl Scouts, is also helpful.

It may be easier for a beginning patroller to get a job at a small ski area than at a large one, Commins says; a move to a larger resort will be facilitated by experience. Although the pay is not as good in smaller ski areas as at larger ones, smaller operations offer a more low-key environment for persons preferring such a setting.

College is not necessary for this career, but Commins suggests that it can help for advancement or as something to fall back on in case of injuries. Commins studied journalism with a minor in art, and although he did not obtain a degree, he has put his journalism studies to good use—his first book, *Ski Patroller,* was published in 1990, and he has written numerous articles for *Ski Patrol Magazine,* the official publication of the National Ski Patrol.

The ski season runs from mid-November to the third week in April. Persons who work as patrollers year after year (and many do, says Commins) work on summer jobs such as construction work (the season begins just as the ski slopes are closing), river-rafting guiding, fishing guiding, or as tennis or golf pros.

For twelve years Commins drove trucks on highway construction crews during the off-season, but for the last six years he has been fortunate enough to work at Grand Targhee year-round on ski-related work. During the off-season Commins does small construction projects such as carpentry and electrical work. One summer he supervised a major landscaping project. To improve the ski trails, he trims trees and blasts rocks.

Commins is enthusiastic about his job: "I like the skiing time, working outdoors, helping others, and making a safer skiing environment. I like the camaraderie of working with a group of people who all like their jobs and work well together. This is mostly a low-pressure job, except when there are injuries."

Like most jobs, ski patrolling does have some negative aspects. The major one that Commins cites is dealing with persons who break the rules. Some ski too fast, endangering themselves and others, while others want to ski in areas that are closed to the public—a misdemeanor in Wyoming.

Skiers often have knee problems. Commins has had operations on both knees and knows all too well what knee pain is like. Before and during the season he rides an indoor bicycle to keep his knees in shape.

Although pay is improving, ski patrollers do not receive high wages; supervisors do receive better pay. "Ski patrollers have to balance the money they earn," says Commins. "Generally, they earn more in their summer jobs."

People who seek out this career should be able to work well in a team and like to help people, according to Commins. Good verbal communications skills are essential and the ability to do "nuts-and-bolts work" is helpful. Patrollers must also be able to handle the stress when injuries occur and make decisions quickly in a crisis. Commins says that the outlook for work in ski patrolling is good; there are openings every year.

See Ski Patrolling, page 153.

Tourboat Captain
Tim Jones

How did it happen that Tim Jones, with a bachelor's degree in journalism and years of experience on newspapers including the *Chicago Tribune* and the *Wall Street Journal,* became a tourboat captain in Alaska?

It all started when Jones took a vacation in Alaska in 1973. He fell in love with the area. "It was the romance and the frontier aspect of the wild country that drew me," Jones says enthusiastically. As luck would have it, he was offered a job in Alaska on that same trip.

And so he moved to Alaska, working in Anchorage for seven years, first as news editor of the *Anchorage Daily News* and then with *Alaska Magazine.* But he still wasn't where he wanted to be, and a boat trip to Prince William Sound set his course. "We have this humorous saying that 'Anchorage is the closest big city to Alaska,'" Jones laughs. "I absolutely fell in love with Prince William Sound. It has everything—mountains, ocean, glacier—and you could explore it for years."

Jones also fell in love with boating, and within a year he had his own boat that he used for exploring the sound. Building on sailing knowledge from his youth, Jones learned how to navigate this boat by reading about the subject and practicing. But this still wasn't enough, so he began to save money so he could cut loose from his life in the city.

In early 1980 he achieved his goal. He quit his writing job, moved to a cabin he had built seven miles from the nearest road, and wrote a book. By summer he had obtained a small captain's license—"By that time I had enough time driving a boat to qualify for a Coast Guard license," he comments—and started working driving boats.

"It didn't pay much money," Jones admits, "and I had to get jobs in the winter to make ends meet." Nevertheless, he was able to live very simply in his cabin. "It was wonderful for me. But not everybody is cut out to live that way."

Two years later Jones began working for a larger company, and by 1984 he became captain of a tourboat. He was actually a jack-of-all-trades on the boat, functioning also as chief engineer and tour guide. "My wide range of interests helped me in working up the tour guide narration," he explains. "I did my own research and prepared the narration." It was a life that Jones enjoyed.

"It's really something to be a part of the boat world as a professional," he says enthusiastically. "The camaraderie among the people who work in the harbor is just great." He also enjoyed the trips. "Every trip was different. You saw different species of wildlife on each trip."

The job had its down side, however. The greatest drawback for Jones was the fact that the tourboat was confined to a specific route during the tour, and he "couldn't get to other and exciting parts of the sound." Also, being a jack-of-all-trades had its tedious aspects. "There was a lot of maintenance in taking care of a large boat that has to meet Coast Guard specifications and has to run all the time," Jones confides. "Some people also got really tired by the end of the season. One summer I worked for 120 days without any time off."

For anyone who aspires to this type of life, Jones advises realistically, "It's important to be prepared not to make a lot of money. The tourist trade is very seasonal, and in Alaska summer is a short season. To make ends meet you need to either live simply in the off-seasons or take a job.

"I adopted a philosophy I call 'creative poverty.' I didn't take any job that had no specific ending time, and I saved half of the money I earned. Thus for every day I worked I knew I was buying a day of freedom."

During the winters Jones wrote. He has written three books. The first two are about the Iditarod, the Alaska sled-dog race from Anchorage to Nome. The first is a general look at the race, and the second was co-written with the first female Iditarod winner. The third book is a departure, a book of nursery rhymes written for high-quality photographs of Alaska taken by a friend. He also managed a local paper, the *Nome Nugget,* during an off-season.

Jones's goal was to enjoy life and have time to do what he wanted to do: write. The Exxon *Valdez* spill temporarily ended this life for Jones. He had an accident while assisting with the cleanup and left the tourboat life.

"This oil spill has ruined Prince William Sound for me and many other Alaskans," Jones explains. "Between the oil fouling the sound and the many people who came in for the cleanup [which he says has not been effective], the sound has changed." Although he still loves the sound, he hadn't been out on it at all in the summer of 1991—for the first summer in ten years—and it doesn't draw him as it used to.

Jones now works for a salmon hatchery in the sound as fishing vessel administrator. His major responsibility is to co-ordinate a program that would use local fishing boats to assist in the event of another oil spill. "I like the fact that this job would allow me to make something happen if there were another oil spill," he says.

Jones speaks of his tourboat days nostalgically and says he and his wife are planning to return to a life like that someday.

See The Tourism Industry, page 155.

*"***F***or me the preservation and celebration of the natural world is a continual concern and the underlying motive for virtually all of my art."*

Robert Bateman

Indoor Careers with an Outdoor Twist

Many people who passionately love the outdoors find great satisfaction in careers that are largely spent indoors but have the outdoors as the vital ingredient. Indoor skills are required for these types of work, but they build upon knowledge of the outdoors as well as a love of the outdoors and outdoor life.

Artists who concentrate on nature and wildlife subjects spend their working time inside while focusing on the outdoors; they may also spend research time outside. Teachers who teach subjects related to the outdoors, such as geography, environmental sciences, or agronomy, often do some research outside in preparation or as part of their work.

Writing and editing on outdoor topics also mainly involve working inside but spotlight outside topics. Here, a keen knowledge of the outdoors is required, as is the ability to conduct research. In fact, writing can be combined with another career that is not full-time or year-round, such as recreation, to provide a full-time living for an outdoor enthusiast.

Organizations that focus on preserving and maintaining the natural world offer many different types of positions. Often these indoor jobs require some knowledge of, and dedication to, the outdoors.

Owners and workers in stores that supply outdoor equipment, from camping and hiking to scuba diving, may also fall into the category of persons whose interest in and expertise on the outdoors, however narrowly focused, adds to the knowledge they bring to their work and the enjoyment they derive from it.

This chapter concentrates on several careers that require specific skills. Don't let this limit you; rather, use it as a point from which to take off. Use these examples and the other possibilities mentioned to find your own niche.

For example, you may have artistic talent and interest in becoming an artist. If you are not succeeding in a career as an artist, perhaps because of timing, market volatility, or location, you might become involved in gallery management or work as an agent for a painter or group of painters. Here, a knowledge of the field would be a distinct advantage, and you will be able to work in an arena of particular interest to you.

You may have to put together several options to find the work best suited to your own particular mix of skills, interests, and aptitudes. But when you do, the result will be happiness in work that you have chosen.

Wildlife and Nature Art

Salary Range: quite varied and unpredictable
Educational Requirements: art courses are an asset
Employment Outlook: in stable economic times, good for artists with clientele

Wildlife and nature art has almost become a field in itself; unfortunately, however, some art galleries do not consider it a real art. It has blossomed in the twentieth century with the work of such pioneers as John James Audubon and Roger Tory Peterson, who focused exclusively on birds in their paintings. As more persons have become interested in wildlife and nature art, the market has grown and so has the number of artists who can make a living by this art.

In this art field, the approach to the work is as different as the artist doing it. For example, most wildlife artists prefer to work from their own experiences in the field. This means trips to the wild lugging equipment such as cameras and sketchpads. It may also mean long days in the outdoors looking for subjects and frantic moments of photography or sketching before the elusive subject melts away into the wild. Others may use zoos or wildlife preserves, which do not require such an arduous approach to locating the subject matter.

For the person who loves the outdoors, some of the career satisfaction comes from being in the outdoors doing the research. Completion of a work to his or her own standards is another reward. To those who become very successful and can command high prices for their work (as much as $5,000 and up, per piece), another satisfaction comes from the money earned.

To succeed in this career, an obvious requirement is that one be artistically gifted. Without this innate gift, no amount of study and work will compensate and enable one to produce artistic creations that large numbers of the public are willing to buy. Most successful wildlife and nature artists have studied art, and many have studied biology or zoology in college. These courses complement the artistic ability with greater knowledge of animals and birds and their habitats.

Artists frequently enter this field from a full-time job in another, often related, career. This allows them time to develop both their artistic skill and a market for their work. Others may continue to augment their art income with full- or part-time work.

Painting—with acrylics, oils, or watercolors—is probably the most common form of art used by nature and wildlife artists. This art field is fairly varied, however, and also includes ink drawing, illustration, sculpture, carving, photography, and what are often called crafts, such as decorating a napkin holder with a painted bird or notepaper with a batiked wildlife illustration.

See Profiles, pages 182 and 185.

Teaching

Salary Range: for university and college teachers this depends on rank and institution; instructors receive from $21,600 to $24,900, assistant professors about $29,200, associate professors about $37,800, and full professors from $40,000 to $64,800. For secondary-school teachers the average is about $30,000, depending on location and educational background

Educational Requirements: for university and college, doctorate or be completing one; for secondary schools, a bachelor's degree plus additional training or a master's

Employment Outlook: large numbers of university and college faculty who were hired in the expansion of the late 1950s and early 1960s are now retiring so there will be some openings, especially in the sciences; there is a fair demand for secondary-school teachers

Universities and Colleges
Teaching offers a good opportunity to deal with outdoor-related subjects from an indoor location. And for many teaching positions at the university level, an essential component of teaching is research, which often involves work in the outdoors. Teachers of many subjects, such as plant pathology, need to continue to do research to keep up with their field.

Teachers also need to read current literature and attend conferences to learn what others in the field are doing. Writing their research findings in scholarly journals is essential for college and university faculty members; such writing is considered in the decision of whether they receive tenure, or job security.

At the university or college level, teachers need to prepare lectures, laboratory experiments, and exercises; grade exams and papers; and work one-on-one with students as necessary. They may lecture in large halls to classes numbering in the hundreds, conduct seminars, direct laboratory periods, or supervise graduate students in teaching, research, and experiments.

Faculty members usually teach several courses in their department. They are often involved with academic committees relating to the policies of the institution. The amount of time spent on each of these activities will depend on the institution and the individual faculty member.

College teachers generally have flexible schedules. Aside from being available for their classes and institutional meetings, they can organize their time as desired. Depending on their teaching schedule, they may have time off during the summer for research, travel, or personal interests.

Teaching can be intellectually challenging and stimulating, and the flexibility it offers can be very attractive. With tight budgets and possibly declining enrollment, institutions of higher learning are hiring more faculty members on a part-time basis than previously. Many of these part-time personnel also have jobs outside the institution or balance part-time positions in more than one institution. Part-time faculty members usually do not have benefits as part of the contract, however—a definite negative. But part-time jobs may eventually lead to a full-time job. They may also be the answer for someone who wants to spend more working time outside, if that person can locate the right part-time job to complement the part-time faculty position.

In the 1970s and 1980s there was keen competition for faculty positions at universities and colleges. Because many current faculty, hired during university expansion in the late 1950s and 1960s, will be retiring during the 1990s, some positions will open up. Additionally, some academic fields may be expanding because of current problems, such as environment and waste disposal.

Tenure is a permanent contract for which faculty members qualify after having worked for a certain period of time, usually seven years. At the university level, a doctorate is required for tenure. Tenure is granted only if the candidate's teaching, research, and general contribution to the university is favorable and if tenured positions are available. Hiring may take place while completion of the doctorate is in progress, but completion within a certain time limit is essential.

Obtaining a doctorate is usually a matter of four to seven years of full-time study after a bachelor's degree. A dissertation—a major paper reporting on research conducted in an important area of study in the field—must also be completed.

Teaching positions in some university departments, such as art, dance, and law, may require certain qualifications other than a doctorate.

Important qualifications for college and university teaching are intelligence, a mind that questions and analyzes information, and a love of knowledge. Verbal and written communications skills are essential, as is the ability to establish rapport with students. Ability to work without direct supervision is also essential.

Secondary Schools

Secondary-school teachers educate students from grades seven through twelve (in some districts this may be grades five through twelve). They are responsible for teaching certain subjects, either academic classes or skill-demanding courses such as art or woodworking, supervising extracurricular activities, and serving on committees. Secondary-school teaching involves team planning with other teachers, administrators, school counselors, and psychologists. Some involvement with parents and parent groups as well as the community is also important.

Secondary-school teachers must have a good knowledge of the subject or subjects they teach and the ability to communicate that information. Being able to relate well to students and to motivate them to study are other important qualities.

Generally, secondary-school teachers teach between four and seven classes a day. They may also be in charge of a homeroom, where they take attendance, or study halls, where they maintain a quiet atmosphere conducive to study.

Teaching secondary-school students—helping prepare the nation's youth for the twenty-first century—is a challenging and rewarding career. It requires extra time spent during the evenings and weekends in class preparation and grading tests and assignments. Troubles facing many schools, such as drugs and disciplinary problems, can make secondary-school teaching more difficult.

Each state has specific certification requirements for secondary-school teachers. These vary by state, but generally to obtain certification a teacher must have a bachelor's degree in the subject to be taught. Teaching experience and classes in education are usually required; these may be included in the bachelor's degree. Increasingly, a master's degree or study toward one is becoming important for secondary-school teachers. Written or oral exams may also be required. It is important to check the requirements, as well as projected needs, for secondary-school teachers in your state before you embark upon this career.

Secondary-school teachers usually teach classes of between ten and thirty students. They must be able to spend most of the day standing and to speak for a great deal of that time. Teaching hours are generally between 9 A.M. and 3 P.M. Summer months are usually free; many teachers use this time for additional study or to earn extra income. Some teachers use the summer for outdoor work to balance their regular indoor work.

Writing and Editing

Salary Range: extremely varied depending on location, employer, and type of work; from about $18,000 beginning to $35,000 plus; technical writing is most remunerative

Educational Requirements: college usually expected, but demonstrated ability is most important

Employment Outlook: good

The work of writers and editors centers on written communication. Writers produce magazine and newspaper articles, books, newsletters, and radio and television scripts. Editors organize publications, supervise writers, and prepare material for publication or broadcasting.

Writing and editing related to the outdoors offer many possibilities. They can either be the major focus of a career or be combined with a seasonal outdoor career to provide an adequate living. Persons skilled in and interested in the outdoors bring an added dimension to writing and editing material about the outdoors that cannot be matched by those simply working on assignment.

Writers gather information through personal observation and experience, research, and interviews. They then attempt to find the best words through which to convey the information to the reader. For most writers, revising and rewriting are essential in the process of communicating information.

Writers may work on a free-lance basis, although this is easiest for established writers to do. Others may be employed full-time by a particular publication or organization.

While many editors do some writing in addition to rewriting and editing, the major focus for some is the overall content of a publication or a radio or television production. For printed materials, editors may select and assign topics and oversee the production process. For radio or television productions, the editorial function is geared more strictly to the content, and production managers take over the final stages.

Editors may have a number of assistants to help in the publication process. These may include copy editors, who check copy for errors in grammar, punctuation, and spelling; assistant editors, who edit copy for style, agreement with editorial policy, and readability, and may do some rewriting and editing; and editorial assistants, who may assist writers by doing research and verifying facts.

For free-lance work, the necessary requirement is a demonstrated ability to write or edit well. Degrees or education are definite assets, but the proof of ability is in the actual demonstration. For part- or full-time positions with an organization or on a publication, the requirement is usually a college degree; some employers prefer English, journalism, or communications graduates, while others prefer a broad liberal arts background.

Writing and editing are specific skills that require clear and logical expression. Valuable traits for writers include creativity, perseverance, and self-motivation. A wide range of knowledge and intellectual curiosity are also important. Familiarity with word processing is almost essential, and computer publishing knowledge is helpful. Practical writing experience, through high school or college papers, volunteer work, an internship, or free-lance work, is very important in this field.

Editors also often need a knowledge of word processing. For many positions, the judgment and ability to select material for publication and to organize are essential as well. Tact in dealing with others and the ability to advise and assist others in their work are other helpful qualities for editors.

Although the need for writers and editors is expected to increase during the 1990s, competition for jobs and for free-lance work should remain intense because many people are attracted to the field.

Writing and editing jobs can be excellent forums for persons who are concerned about issues of conservation and preservation of natural resources.

See Profile, page 187.

See Profile, page 187.

Conservation and Environmental Organization Work

Salary Range: extremely varied depending on size of organization, location, and position; from about $20,000 for clerical workers up to $150,000 plus for executive directors

Educational Requirements: from high school to doctorate, depending on position

Employment Outlook: good, although a recession will cause organizations to tighten their belts

Many associations and organizations center on conservation, the environment, and other issues related to the outdoors. They offer many kinds of positions and a good forum for outdoor concerns. These associations come in all sizes; the types and scope of positions at each organization directly relate to its size and purpose.

Members of these organizations have a common interest or background in a certain subject or profession such as wildlife, the environment, or conservation. Members join because of interest or to increase their expertise. Average staff size is between ten and thirty employees, although some organizations have many more staffers, with very specialized functions.

Informing members is a major function of all of these associations. Many also work to influence policy or events. The various tasks association staffers may perform include writing special studies; publishing magazines, books, newspapers, or news releases; giving public speeches or lobbying on special issues; arranging meetings, seminars, and conventions; handling marketing and sales functions; and arranging shows and exhibitions.

Association positions include executive director, writers and editors, legislative staff members or lobbyists, public relations personnel, information gatherers and researchers, and fund-raisers.

An example of a large organization with varied career positions available around the United States and abroad is The Nature Conservancy. A commitment to conservation is important for all jobs with this organization, whose major purpose is to preserve natural diversity. This is done by conserving lands and waters that support various species of wildlife and plants, especially those species that may be threatened with extinction. Most of the Conservancy's more than one thousand staffers work in office settings. The corporate headquarters is in metropolitan Washington, D.C., but only some two hundred work at this office; the rest work in the four regional offices, in state offices, and on the Conservancy preserves.

The Nature Conservancy has seven major divisions with specific responsibilities. The Resources Division includes communications, essential to publicize the mission and accomplishments of the Conservancy; development, or fund-raising; trade lands, or gifts of real estate; planned giving; and government relations, or lobbying, which, although not a major Conservancy effort, monitors national and state legislation affecting the organization's concerns or the natural areas it protects.

The Science Division is in charge of developing and maintaining extensive databases on the flora and fauna of the Western Hemisphere. Many of these jobs are for field scientists in Heritage programs, which may mean outdoor work gathering data on plants and animals and assisting in land-use planning and assessing environmental impact.

The Latin America Division works toward the Conservancy's overall goal of preserving biological diversity by working with independent conservation organizations in Latin America. The Stewardship Division oversees the Conservancy preserves and the projects that work toward maintaining biological diversity. The Administration and Training Division performs personnel, training, and administrative functions. The Data Systems, Finance, and Accounting Division gives computer support and assistance with systems development. And the Regional Office Division manages the Conservancy's business in each of the four regional areas from head offices in Boston, Minneapolis, San Francisco, and Chapel Hill, North Carolina.

The Conservancy also has part-time, seasonal, intern, and volunteer positions. An employment hotline (703-247-3721) is updated every week with job vacancies. Regional and state Conservancy offices also have employment information.

The nation boasts many different associations and organizations. The largest single grouping of national and international organizations in the United States is in the Washington, D.C., area. Other top locations are Boston and New York City, but associations can be found all around the country. Directories can assist in finding associations or organizations that may be of interest to you.

Museum Work

Salary Range: extremely varied depending on the size of the museum; curator positions from about $25,000 to $103,000
Educational Requirements: bachelor's degree; for some positions, graduate study.
Employment Outlook: fair

Museums house the things a society values—historic objects, animals, plants, paintings—so that the public may be educated and informed. These collections of treasures require experts in different fields to organize and maintain them. For some museums, such as a museum of natural history, many of the specialized positions require knowledge of the outdoors or outdoor-related information.

The museum curator acquires pieces, develops and arranges displays, does research, and writes reports. Museum positions require quite specialized backgrounds. Large museums may have a curator for each field of study represented in the museum, with other staffers to build, repair, and care for the displays. In a smaller setting, the curator will do all of this work.

Among the technical staffers in larger museums are conservators, who regulate temperatures and lighting to keep valuable objects well preserved. Taxidermists stuff animal skins for displays in natural history museums. Restorers who can repair worn or damaged objects may also be hired in museums.

Other museum positions include administrators in personnel and accounting, who keep the operation running, and important support functions such as guides, shop clerks, and guards. The director, usually an expert in a specific field, oversees, plans, and sets policy for the whole museum operation.

Specific skills necessary for work in museums depend on the function to be performed. Many positions demand quite specific scientific knowledge or skills such as writing and editing. Salaries vary tremendously depending on the type and size of the museum and the specific work and background requirements.

Some new museums are being built, which will open up additional museum jobs. A decrease in federal funding for museums, however, will reduce the number of new museums and expansions. Museum jobs, especially in the larger ones such as the Smithsonian Institution in Washington, D.C., are very attractive. Competition for these jobs is quite intense.

Resources
Conservation Organization Work

Careers: The Nature Conservancy, brochure about administrative, support, and some highly technical positions in one specific organization, available from The Nature Conservancy, 1815 North Lynn Street, Arlington, VA 22209 (703-841-5300).

The following two directories list specific organizations.

Lanier-Graham, Susan D. *The Nature Directory: A Guide to Environmental Organizations.* New York: Walker and Company, 1991. This book has a short chapter dealing with environmental problems, an introduction to about one hundred environmental organizations, a brief "guide to personal involvement," and listings of books and government agencies.

Conservation Directory, 1991. Washington, DC: National Wildlife Federation, 1991. This directory, updated annually, lists organizations, agencies, and officials concerned with natural resource use and management. This extensive listing includes governmental and nongovernmental organizations at state, national, and international levels. The 1992 edition, item number 79559, is available for $18.00 plus $3.95 shipping charge from National Wildlife Federation, 1400 Sixteenth Street, N.W., Washington, DC 20036-2266.

Museum Work

Information on museum careers is available from the American Association of Museums; for listing and prices write to American Association of Museums, Technical Information Services, 1225 Eye Street, N.W., Washington, DC 20005 (202-289-1818).

Nature Artist
Robert Bateman

"My goal in life has always been to live in or near nature and not in some high-rise apartment in the city. Supporting myself with my art was never a goal," confides internationally known artist Robert Bateman, who describes himself as "an artist who's interested in nature."

Bateman's "meal ticket" to this quality of life was teaching; he taught high school art and geography for twenty years before becoming a full-time painter. Although he enjoyed teaching ("I couldn't see why they paid me all that money to have fun talking to a bunch of teenagers"), Bateman admits, "I would come home from teaching and get on with my life: doing art and having adventures in nature."

Bateman has garnered an international reputation for realism in portraying animals and nature. In some paintings, the wildlife subject almost appears to be going off the picture or is hard to locate. The care he gives to the natural settings in his paintings shows his passionate love of nature. Bateman's concern for the natural world is also shown in his involvement in international and local environmental causes. He gives about five to ten speeches a year—speeches that he characterizes as "getting more and more militantly environmental."

Bateman does not take himself or his success too seriously. In fact, this personable and outgoing artist has a problem with the word *success*. "To me," he says matter-of-factly, "success is how well I do each painting and how I'm thought of by my peers and people whose opinions I respect."

This Canadian's love of nature began in his youth and was nurtured through family interests, naturalist clubs, and summers working on wildlife research or geological field parties. Bateman has a bachelor's degree in geography and a high school teaching certificate, plus many years of art classes. Early in his teaching career, he traveled around the world in a Land Rover. He and his naturalist friends augmented their trip money by collecting specimens for Canadian, U.S., and

British museums. These travels and the two years he spent teaching geography in Africa have influenced the subjects of his paintings.

Patience is the first quality Bateman cites as important for artists. Also important, he adds, is "the ability to really look, not just superficially glance, at something." Perhaps the most important trait, however, is one he often finds lacking in budding artists. "It is important to be a tough and observant critic of the project you're working on. I'm just amazed at the things young artists don't notice about their own work.

"I would advise aspiring artists to get a meal ticket so they don't have to paint for the market," Bateman continues. "It's dangerous to start selling too young; artists may start imitating themselves instead of going on to find their own artistic voice. Art is a unique and special individual expression. Artists who paint for the market too early may put a ceiling on their creativity and never rise above mediocrity."

Bateman divides his time among painting, research, and book tours. "I have a specific routine when I'm painting," he explains. "I work from nine o'clock in the morning until noon. I take a walk before lunch, and after lunch I have a nap and coffee before I get back to painting. I have another walk before dinner. When the weather's nice, I eat outside." The painting routine gives him one or two hours a day outdoors, although he has a magnificent view of nature from his studio window. His research is usually conducted on camping trips, with 100 percent of his time spent outdoors.

On book tours, Bateman's schedule consists of an early start for a radio or TV interview, a newspaper interview, catching the noon crowds at a bookstore, another newspaper interview after lunch, catching the evening crowds in a bookstore over dinner hour, and then either a lecture or traveling on to the next town in the evening. Bateman's most recent book tour publicized *Robert Bateman: An Artist in Nature,* published in 1990.

About the business end of painting, Bateman says, "I have had a charmed life." He adds, "I'm hopeless at anything to do with selling and business. If I had to sell my own paintings, I would still be giving them away." His first show in 1967 sold out on opening night, and the demand for his art has remained constant ever since. Bateman employs an assistant who handles charity, interview, and photography requests, arranges tour itineraries, and serves as a liaison with his publisher.

"The only down side to my career is that I'm getting too much on my plate," Bateman admits. He also concedes that he is "way behind. I have many ideas that I would like to paint." Bateman says that he can't hurry his paintings, however. "They are like whiskey or wine—you can't force them to be ready. When I leave a picture sitting around I see other little strokes that I might not have thought of a month ago."

Although his paintings hang in the private collections of the rich and famous around the world, Bateman remains modest and unpretentious. He remarks philosophically, "It may not continue. I remember reading this slogan: 'No condition is permanent.' The economy is down and my prices are higher. But the only problem if my paintings don't sell would be a bruise to my ego."

See Wildlife and Nature Art, page 170.

Wildlife Sculptor
Ott Jones

"My ideas and inspiration for my sculptures all come from my time spent in the outdoors. The animals and birds I have done came to be through an experience with them in the outdoors," relates Ott Jones, a full-time wildlife sculptor since 1983. "The outdoors has always been an important part of my life."

As a youth growing up in Spokane, Washington, Jones hunted and fished with his father. After graduating from college, he spent three summers in Alaska as a fishing guide and a year on the Alaskan pipeline working as a welder's helper. "Alaska has been the biggest influence on my career," he indicates. "Besides getting much inspiration and many ideas from the abundant wildlife, I was very fortunate in meeting many contacts and collectors, which allowed me to go full-time."

Jones recommends that artists use three approaches to developing clientele: advertising, art shows, and art galleries. "I feel an artist benefits most by developing his or her own clientele list. This takes time, of course, but word of mouth is the best advertising and one's list will grow."

Artists should be as professional as possible in setting up every phase of the business, advises Jones, who now works in Bozeman, Montana. Essential pieces of the business setup are the inventory, the books, and show schedules. "One must plan out how many pieces of art will be released, at what price ranges, and at what time of the year."

Research is an important part of his work, says Jones. The research materials he uses in creating a sculpture include his photographs, library books, videotapes, study skins, and live models. "In researching a piece, much of my time is spent afield studying and observing the animal in its natural habitat," he adds.

Jones has some very specific advice for young artists. "I would say the best way for a young artist to polish his or her skills would be to first do an apprenticeship under a well-known artist in whatever specific type of art he or she is interested in.

Second, participate in as many workshops as possible. And third, practice and do as much artwork as possible. An artist must find his or her style and technique and strive to perfect that. Like all things, the more you practice, the better you will become."

See Wildlife and Nature Art, page 170.

Outdoor Writer and Trail Builder
Bob Birkby

"I got interested in the outdoors through my father, leader of the local scout troop, and hundreds of campouts in the corn," relates Bob Birkby, an Iowa native who now works as an outdoor writer and a trail builder. The six summers he worked at Philmont, a Boy Scout camp in northern New Mexico, as a backcountry trail crew foreman and later as director of conservation added to his love of the outdoors. "In addition to being great fun," Birkby recalls, "those summers taught me the basics of wilderness leadership and also gave me a fair expertise in trail construction and maintenance."

Birkby earned bachelor's and master's degrees in English and spent three years teaching writing at Southwest Missouri State University. "I was well on the way to a lifetime as a college professor," Birkby says, "but there was the small matter of the Appalachian Trail. It was just, well, *out there,* demanding to be hiked. In fact, there was a whole lot of *out there* out there, and the confines of classrooms, libraries, and faculty meetings were bringing on major career claustrophobia."

So Birkby quit his teaching job, hiked the Appalachian Trail from Maine to Georgia, and headed west, arriving in Seattle about the time his savings ran out.

He first wrote a novel, but he decided it was not worthy of print. Then he began writing short articles about the odd jobs that had paid his rent. In search of another odd job, he came in contact with the Student Conservation Association (SCA), which immediately offered him a job supervising a high school trail crew. "It was a perfect match for me—the chance to teach, to use my trail construction skills, and to spend extended periods in the backcountry," explains Birkby. "Over the years, I've supervised SCA programs along the Buffalo River in Arkansas, in the Nez Perce National Forest in Idaho, at the bottom of the Grand Canyon, and in Yellowstone, Glacier, and

Kings Canyon National Parks. In 1990 I directed the SCA exchange program with the Soviet Union, spending the first half of the summer in Yellowstone and the second half in the national parks of Latvia and Estonia."

Birkby is also an instructor in the SCA Wilderness Work Skills Program and a writer for the Boy Scouts of America. Using his contacts from previous work with the Boy Scouts, he got a job writing an eighty-page merit badge pamphlet under a very tight deadline, and, says Birkby, "The BSA and I were on our way." He has done other work for the Boy Scouts, including writing columns for *Boys' Life* magazine, revising the camping and hiking merit badge pamphlets, and editing new editions of the *Scout Fieldbook* and the *Boy Scout Handbook*. Along the way he has written two other books—one a how-to book, *Learn How to Canoe in One Day*—and is currently writing another book for the Boy Scouts.

"When I left teaching, I had hopes of finding a career that involved writing and outdoor adventures, but I didn't have a clue where to begin finding it," Birkby confides. "Now I write six or seven months of the year, and then when the snow melts out of the mountains, I head for places high and wild. There have been years when my outdoor work in the summer has supported a winter of writing, and years when what I earn as a writer has funded my summer adventures.

"The world of outdoor writing has its own wicked difficulties. Over the years I've known lots of people who wanted to be/were becoming/were convinced they were outdoor writers. The older I get, though, the fewer people I know who are my age and still writing. It is a career with a brutal attrition rate.

"When asked if she enjoyed writing, Gertrude Stein said no, but she enjoyed having written. I think that is at the heart of outdoor writing careers—from the outside it sure seems like an exciting way to make a living (and in fact there are times when it is). The reality, though, is that it is a discipline just as demanding and harsh as mountaineering. To survive as a writer, you've got to have an innate love for how words fit together—you've got to *like* playing with the language. You also need to have something to write about, and that means getting in the field, seeing what there is to see, and developing some clear opinions. Hardest of all, you have to hunker down and just do it—sit at a desk and hammer out the work for days, weeks, and months at a time.

"There is no typical career path to becoming a writer/trail builder. Nor is there a typical day's work (last week I got up, wrote until I couldn't see straight, went to bed; this week I flew to Latvia, built rustic hiking bridges, went to bed).

"Like a full-time mountaineer, a writer takes on the responsibility for inventing his own career. That can be extremely scary at times. For many people, the uncertainty is too much to deal with. But when the pieces fall in place and the adventures and the writing mesh into one glorious flow, there is no better way to live."

See Writing and Editing, page 175.

*"**T**he greater the number of job-hunting avenues you use, the greater the likelihood that you will find a job."*

Richard Nelson Bolles,
What Color Is Your Parachute?

Some Tips on the Job Search

By the time you read this chapter you most likely will have focused on a specific career or career area. Once you have reached that point, it is helpful to do some additional research before you begin your job search in earnest. Look at books and other resources that cover the particular career in greater detail. Especially valuable, if you have no work or volunteer experience in the career, are informational interviews with persons currently working in this field. This will help round out your knowledge of that career and will also give you contacts who may be helpful when you begin your job search.

This chapter will review some of the critical aspects of this part of the job search process and point the way to additional and more detailed information.

Writing Your Résumé

A résumé is an essential job search tool, and preparing one is one of the first steps to take in the job search. Remember that a résumé is a selective summary of your skills, abilities, and work and study experiences. It is not a life history, but it should provide enough critical information about your background to interest a potential employer in interviewing you.

Writing your own résumé, instead of hiring a résumé service to prepare one for you, is a valuable part of the job search process.

191

Although résumé writing takes effort, it is well worth the time; it is excellent preparation for the job interview when you need to focus on your background. If you do consult an outside source to assist you in writing your résumé, be sure that you are actively involved in the process.

In writing a résumé, make certain to include all of your pertinent skills and experience to ensure that you are presenting yourself as favorably as possible. Because a résumé is usually the first representation of yourself to a potential employer, it must be clear, concise, and well written. Before beginning to write the actual résumé, take some time to write down information you think should be included. Organize your information under the following headings.

Career Objective. Your career objective, a simple statement of the kind of career you are seeking, should also include brief information about your skills or background. Some persons do not feel comfortable writing a career objective and prefer to give a skills summary. The value of this information is that it helps to focus your résumé and gives your background in brief.

Skills and Work Experience. Write out your work experience and then elaborate, giving the skills used in each job. It is important to describe what you actually did or accomplished. If you are a recent graduate or are changing careers, you can include summer, part-time, or volunteer positions as well as extracurricular activities. The focus here should not be on any job title, which can often be misleading, but on the job content. What actual skills did the job entail?

Your résumé should show the skills you have used and give examples of your accomplishments. In detailing your skills and accomplishments, use action verbs. The many excellent résumé books available usually give comprehensive listings of such verbs.

If you are changing careers, remember that you may use some of the same skills you utilized in previous work. For example, you may be moving from a supervisory position to an editing and writing position; many supervisory positions involve writing and editing, and they also require good organizational and decision-making skills—skills that are certainly necessary for editing and writing positions.

Education. Give your educational background, listing any degrees and the major or concentration. You may also want to list major courses and/or your thesis title; if you don't have a great deal of work experience in the field, this information may be especially important.

Awards and Honors. List any awards, special recognitions, or honors you have received. On your résumé itself, you may include all of these or be selective, listing only those specifically related to your career field or those showing significant achievement.

Interests and Hobbies. Sometimes interests and hobbies have a direct bearing on your career goals and should be included in a résumé. They also help round out your presentation of yourself and, in the case of jobs that may use other aspects of a person's life experiences, give prospective employers a more complete idea of your background. But don't use these on a résumé to the exclusion of information that may be more directly career related.

After writing out this information, you may want to check with close friends and family members to see if you have left out anything of importance. Getting the perspective of others who know you well can be quite helpful in working through this somewhat tedious aspect of résumé writing.

When writing the actual résumé, keep in mind that it is essential to use correct grammar. It is wise to consult a few of the many excellent résumé books when you begin writing the final draft. There you can find many samples of different types of résumés. The Resources section at the end of the chapter includes some recommended books. Many of the job search books listed at the end of chapter 1 also have helpful résumé sections.

Remember that there is no one correct way to write a résumé: Every employer who reads a résumé has different preferences. But these general principles should guide you through résumé preparation. Additionally, you must feel comfortable with the end product; your résumé is about your unique skills and experiences, so use a format that presents the unique person you are to best advantage.

Types of Résumés

The two basic résumé types are *functional* and *chronological*. The chronological résumé organizes work and educational experiences in reverse chronological order. The standard format gives the employer and the job title plus a brief description of the job content. It is most commonly used for persons changing positions in the same field.

The functional résumé emphasizes skills and the content or function of previous work, volunteer, or personal experience. It is usually used by persons who are changing careers and want to emphasize skills they have gained through volunteer work or other related experience. Employers often do not like functional résumés because they tend to obscure the work history.

If you like the idea of emphasizing skills and past accomplishments, you could consider using a functional format that includes past employment, usually called a modified functional résumé. The advantage of this type of résumé is that the focus is squarely where it should be—on your demonstrated skills.

Cover Letters

Always include a cover letter with any résumé, whether you are sending the résumé in response to a job advertisement or as part of a mailing to possible employers. A cover letter must be written in correct business style with no grammatical errors and must be produced by typewriter or word processor, never handwritten.

The purpose of a cover letter is to interest an employer in reading the résumé, so it must be interesting and to the point. The letter must explain why the résumé is being sent—for example, in response to a job ad, because the organization was recommended to you by someone (give the name if it is a person of influence), or because you are looking for work in this field. If the letter is in response to an advertised job, focus on the particular skills and experiences that relate to this job.

The first paragraph should explain your purpose in sending the résumé. The main body of the letter should describe you and tell how your unique skills and abilities could fill the employer's needs. Be specific in telling how you have used your skills to accomplish a certain goal. The closing paragraph should lead to action. You may wish to give a time when you will contact the employer rather than saying that you look forward to hearing from them. You could also state your willingness to send more information.

Creative Job Search

It is essential to use creativity in your job search and employ many strategies. Apply for jobs listed in newspapers, association or trade publications, and the publications listed in appendix I of this book, but don't let this be the sole focus of your job search.

Also approach contacts you may have from summer, volunteer, or part-time jobs. To expand or develop a network of contacts, conduct informational interviews; these can yield information about a career in addition to contacts in the field.

The purpose of an informational interview at this stage of your job search is to ask for advice or suggestions on your search strategy. To arrange for an interview, contact someone who is in the career that interests you. Tell this person that you would like some suggestions on your job search strategy, and ask for a few minutes of his or her time. Bring a list of questions to the interview and conduct yourself very professionally. Ask for names of other persons in this field whom you could contact.

Don't ask for a job in this interview, but be prepared with a résumé in case one is requested or a job possibility is mentioned. After the interview, send a letter of thanks, including a résumé if you haven't already left one. You may want to contact these persons later in your job search to let them know that you are now looking for a job in the field.

In addition to good career information, this strategy yields good contacts in the field. If these contacts were impressed with you during the interview, they may be glad to help you when you let them know you're actively searching for a job. Their recommendation of you would be invaluable, because most managers place more faith in the word of people they know than in the hiring process.

Through these contacts, you may hear of positions before they are advertised, when there is less competition. Informational interviews will also help you to become more comfortable in interview situations; this can yield dividends when you interview for jobs later on.

In addition to consciously working to establish a network by conducting informational interviews, you may locate job possibilities by using the network you already have. Speak with family members, friends, professors, and contacts from part-time, summer, or volunteer work.

Joining the appropriate association and attending its workshops and conferences is another way to network, gain contacts in the field, and learn about job possibilities. Jobs are often listed in association newsletters or journals.

Another strategy for finding jobs is to mail résumés to carefully selected employers. Target organizations or companies that have the type of positions you are seeking, and send the résumé to the person who supervises that position. Research to obtain this person's name; it is good to direct your résumé to a person by name instead of simply mailing it to a position title. Some directories have this information, or the switchboard operator of the company may be able to give you the name. These carefully targeted mailings can lead to interviews and more networking possibilities or to actual jobs.

The Job Interview

Many people find the job interview quite frightening. Good preparation should help to make this important step in the job search process much less intimidating. It is also helpful to keep in mind the purpose of the job interview, which is basically for the candidate and the employer to assess each other and decide if this is a good job fit. This means that you, the candidate, are also interviewing the employer. You probably were invited for an interview because your "paper trail"—your letter and résumé—seemed to fit the qualifications the employer had in mind for this position. Employers interview to make certain that there is a fit between a candidate's professional background and work experience and the job that is available. They also want to assess your personality and decide whether it will be compatible with the company.

As you prepare for a job interview, try to learn as much as you can about the department in which the opening exists, including its responsibilities and functions. Also try to learn about the personalities of the potential employer (for example, whether it is very rigidly hierarchical with all decisions and initiatives coming from the top, or whether there is room for individual initiative) and of the person who would be your supervisor.

This research will help you to be more relaxed as you go into the interview. It will also help you formulate questions to obtain more information about the employer, evaluate the employer, and decide whether you want to work for that company. Additionally, your knowledge about the employer will be evident by the questions you ask during the interview. The interviewer will be impressed by your research as an indication of your desire to work for his or her company.

Before the interview, review your skills and be ready to give specific examples of ways your skills could benefit the employer. Be prepared for open-ended questions such as "Tell me about yourself." The employer is not looking for your life history but for pertinent information about you related to the job in question.

Most job search books and interview books have lists of the type of questions generally asked in interviews. It's good to check these out and formulate answers to them in preparation for the interview.

Don't worry if you are nervous about interviewing. As you have more interviews, this aspect of job seeking will become more comfortable. Besides, if you are too relaxed, you may not do your best in the interview. Practicing with a friend before the interview can help calm you and prepare you for formulating your thoughts on the spot.

So prepare well for the interview, learning all you can about the employer ahead of time and reviewing the skills and accomplishments that you will stress in the interview. Then go and do your best. Know realistically that you will not be offered all jobs for which you interview, and likely you will discover that not all of these jobs or employers are quite what you were looking for, either. In addition, competition is keen for many jobs, and many qualified persons may have applied. So don't think that not being offered a job reflects negatively on you. Work to maintain your self-confidence during your job search, which may last longer than you anticipate.

Reading about interviews in some of the many interview or job search books can be helpful as you prepare. But don't build interviewing up to be more difficult than it really is. There is no one right way to interview; as with a résumé, each employer is looking for different things, so what will impress one person will not impress another.

Resources

Résumé Books

Good, C. Edward. *Does Your Résumé Wear Blue Jeans? The Book on Résumé Preparation.* Charlottesville, VA: Blue Jeans Press, 1987.

Krannich, Ronald L. *High Impact Résumés and Letters: How to Communicate Your Qualifications to Employers.* Manassas, VA: Impact Publications, 1988.

Interview Books

Medley, H. Anthony. *Sweaty Palms: The Neglected Art of Being Interviewed.* Berkeley, CA: Ten Speed Press, 1984.

Pettus, Theodore. *One on One: Win the Interview, Win the Job.* New York: Random House, 1981.

Yate, Martin J. *Knock 'Em Dead: With Great Answers to Tough Interview Questions.* Holbrook, MA: Adams, Box, 1985.

General Job Search Books

See the Resources section in chapter 1. Many of these books give information about all aspects of the job search.

Job Listings

Job listings can help you find full-time and short-term jobs and internships. The following listings are those that will be of most interest to persons looking for outdoor or outdoor-related careers. Many of these are publications that are available by subscription. It may be wise to purchase one copy before subscribing to make certain that a particular publication will be helpful in your search.

The CEIP Fund

The CEIP Fund, formerly the Center for Environmental Intern Programs, assists in locating internships and short-term professional environmental jobs. A fee is charged; persons are encouraged to apply several months before they are available, for maximum opportunities. Also available is *The Complete Guide to Environmental Careers,* an excellent book that covers fairly thoroughly the range of careers involved with the environment. Write to The CEIP Fund, Inc., 68 Harrison Ave., Boston, MA 02111-1907.

Environmental Opportunities

Environmental Opportunities is a monthly bulletin that lists employment openings throughout the United States under the following categories: teaching, administration, fisheries/biology/ecology/wildlife, horticulture (primarily educational), outdoor education, nature center, research, organizational, and seasonal positions and internships. Subscriptions are available for six months, one year, and two years from *Environmental Opportunities,* P.O. Box 4957, Arcata, CA 95521 (707-839-4640).

Jobs Available

Jobs Available: A Listing of Employment Opportunities in the Public Sector is a bulletin that includes environmental, engineering, conservation, sanitation, and planning in addition to other public sector positions. The western edition includes states from Illinois and Texas west. A yearly subscription is available from *Jobs Available,* P.O. Box 1040, Modesto, CA 95353 (209-571-2120).

National Association of Interpretation

The National Association of Interpretation offers several services for career, seasonal, part-time, and internship employment opportunities in interpretation, environmental education, and related fields.

Call Dial-a-Job (303-491-7410) for a recording of career, seasonal, and part-time positions available. It runs from ten to thirty minutes and is updated weekly.

Call Dial-an-Internship (303-491-6784) for a recording of internship openings, updated weekly, which runs for five to twenty minutes.

The listings give complete information about the employer, job location, title of position, minimum qualifications, brief statement of responsibilities, salary, application closing date, contact person, and phone number. A printed copy of any week's listings from either Dial-a-Job or Dial-an-Internship may be purchased from National Association of Interpretation, P.O. Box 1892, Fort Collins, CO 80522 (303-491-6434).

JOBSource

JOBSource is a computerized job program designed to give job seekers access to a large data bank of job opportunities. Announcements may be accessed through modem or job searches conducted by staffers of Computerized Employment Systems, Inc. (CESI). A number of colleges and universities also subscribe to this service.

Job categories include agricultural sciences, biological sciences, botany, camp personnel, engineering, environmental education/ interpretation/naturalists, fisheries, forestry, geology, horticulture, hydrology/water quality, microbiology, natural resources (multidisciplinary), natural sciences (multidisciplinary), park/forest ranger and patrol, park administration/management/planning, range sciences, recreation, soil sciences, wildlife biology, and zoology. Jobs are available from across the country and in a broad range of possibilities. Further information is available from Computerized Employment Systems, Inc., 1720 West Mulberry Unit B9, Ft. Collins, CO 80521 (303-493-1779).

The Job Seeker

The Job Seeker is a job-listing publication specializing in the environmental and natural resources fields. It includes private, local, state, and federal vacancies from around the country and gives fairly complete information about the job. It is published twice a month. Subscription rates available for summer, three months, six months, and one year. Contact *The Job Seeker,* Route 2, Box 16, Warrens, WI 54666 (608-378-4290).

The Western Environmental Jobletter

The Western Environmental Jobletter (WEJ) is a monthly newsletter listing environmental job openings—career, internship, seasonal, and part-time—for western North America including Alaska, western Canada, and Mexico. Subscription rates available per issue or for six months, one year, or two years. Contact *The Western Environmental Jobletter,* P.O. Box 269, Westcliffe, CO 81252 (719-746-2252 or 719-742-5305).

Earth Work

Earth Work magazine includes the listing formerly published as *Job Scan,* put out by the Student Conservation Association. It contains environmental and natural resource management job opportunities, including professional and entry-level positions as well as internships and seasonal positions. Subscription rates available per issue or for six months or one year. Contact Student Conservation Association, Inc., P.O. Box 550, Charlestown, NH 03603-9985 (603-826-4301).

Environmental Job Opportunities Bulletin

The *Environmental Job Opportunities Bulletin* lists environmental jobs throughout the United States. It is free on the University of Wisconsin-Madison campus; otherwise a fee is charged for the ten issues per year. Contact *Environmental Job Opportunities,* Institute for

202 · APPENDIX I

Environmental Studies, University of Wisconsin-Madison, 550 North Park Street, 15 Science Hall, Madison, WI 53706 (608-263-3185).

Environmental Communicator

Environmental Communicator is a magazine listing some employment opportunities in environmental jobs. Available from North American Association for Environmental Education, P.O. Box 400, Troy, OH 45373 (513-698-6493).

Sources of Labor Market Information

For detailed labor market reports covering current and future employment in a particular state, contact the chief of labor research and analysis in that state. The following is a listing of titles and addresses.

Alabama
Chief, Research and Statistics
Department of Industrial
    Relations
Industrial Relations Bldg.
649 Monroe St.
Montgomery, AL 36130

Alaska
Chief, Research and Analysis
Employment Security Division
Department of Labor
P.O. Box 3-7000
Juneau, AK 99802-1218

Arizona
Chief, Labor Market
    Information
Research and Analysis

Department of Economic
    Security
P.O. Box 6123
Phoenix, AZ 85005

Arkansas
Chief, Research and Statistics
Employment Security Division
2 Capitol Mall, Rm. 61
Little Rock, AR 72201

California
Chief, Employment Data and
    Research Division
Employment Development
    Department
P.O. Box 826880
Sacramento, CA 94280-0001

Colorado
Chief, Research and Analysis
Division of Employment
Department of Labor and
  Employment
600 Grant St., Ste. 900
Denver, CO 80203-3528

Connecticut
Director, Research and
  Information
Labor Department
200 Folly Brook Blvd.
Wethersfield, CT 06109

Delaware
Chief, Office of Research,
  Planning, and Evaluation
Department of Labor
820 N. French St.
Wilmington, DE 19801

District of Columbia
Chief, Branch of Labor Market
  Information and Analysis
Employment Services
500 C St., N.W.
Washington, DC 20001

Florida
Chief, Research and Statistics
Division of Employment
  Security
2012 Capitol Circle S.E.,
  Hartman Bldg.
Tallahassee, FL 32399-2152

Georgia
Director, Information Systems
Employment Security Agency
Department of Labor
148 International Blvd.
Atlanta, GA 30303

Hawaii
Chief, Research and Statistics
Department of Labor and
  Industrial Relations
830 Punchbowl St.
Honolulu, HI 96813

Idaho
Chief, Research and Analysis
Department of Employment
317 Main St.
Boise, ID 83735

Illinois
Manager, Research and
  Analysis Division
Department of Employment
  Security
Department of Labor
401 S. State St.
Chicago, IL 60605

Indiana
Chief, Research
Employment Security Division
Department of Labor
100 N. Senate Ave., Rm. 1013
Indianapolis, IN 46204

Iowa
Chief, Research and Statistics
Department of Employment
  Services
1000 E. Grand Ave.
Des Moines, IA 50319

Kansas
Chief, Research and Analysis
Department of Human
  Resources
401 Topeka Ave.
Topeka, KS 66603

Kentucky
Chief, Research and Special
  Projects
Department of Human
  Resources
275 E. Main St.
Frankfort, KY 40621

Louisiana
Chief, Research and Statistics
Department of Employment
  Security
P.O. Box 94094
Baton Rouge, LA 70804-9094

Maine
Director, Manpower Research
  Division
Employment Security Com-
  mission
20 Union St., P.O. Box 309
Augusta, ME 04332-0309

Maryland
Director, Research and
  Analysis
Department of Human
  Resources
3111 W. Saratoga St.
Baltimore, MD 21201

Massachusetts
Director, Information and
  Research
Employment and Training
  Department
Hurley Bldg.
Government Center
Boston, MA 02114

Michigan
Director, Research and
  Statistics Division
Employment Security
  Commission
7310 Woodward Ave.
Detroit, MI 48202

Minnesota
Director, Research and
  Statistics Services
Department of Jobs and
  Training
390 N. Robert St.
St. Paul, MN 55101

Mississippi
Chief, Research and Statistics
Employment Security
  Commission

P.O. Box 1699
Jackson, MS 39215

Missouri
Chief, Research and Statistics
Division of Employment
  Security
Department of Labor and
  Industrial Relations
321 E. Dunklin St.
Jefferson City, MO 65101

Montana
Chief, Reports and Analysis
Department of Labor and
  Industry
P.O. Box 1728
Helena, MT 59624

Nebraska
Chief, Research and Statistics
Division of Employment
Department of Labor
P.O. Box 94600
Lincoln, NE 68509

Nevada
Chief, Employment Security
  Research
Employment Security
  Department
500 E. Third St.
Carson City, NV 89713

New Hampshire
Director, Economic Analysis
  and Reports

Department of Employment
  Security
32 S. Main St.
Concord, NH 03301-4857

New Jersey
Director, Division of Planning
  and Research
Department of Labor
John Fitch Plaza, CN 110
Trenton, NJ 08625-0110

New Mexico
Chief, Research and Statistics
Employment Security
  Commission
Department of Labor
P.O. Box 1928
Albuquerque, NM 87103

New York
Director, Division of Research
  and Statistics
Department of Labor
State Campus, Bldg. 12
Albany, NY 12240

North Carolina
Director, Division of Research
  and Statistics
Department of Labor
4 W. Edenton St.
Raleigh, NC 27601

North Dakota
Chief, Research and Statistics
Job Service

P.O. Box 1537
Bismarck, ND 58502

Ohio
Director, Division of Research
and Statistics
Bureau of Employment
Services
145 S. Front St.
Columbus, OH 43216

Oklahoma
Chief, Research and Planning
Division
Employment Security
Commission
2401 N. Lincoln Blvd.
Oklahoma City, OK 73105

Oregon
Assistant Administrator,
Research and Statistics
Bureau of Labor and Industries
1400 S.W. 5th Ave., Ste. 409
Portland, OR 97201

Pennsylvania
Director, Research and
Statistics
Bureau of Employment
Security
Department of Labor and
Industry
Labor and Industry Bldg.
Harrisburg, PA 17120

South Carolina
Director, Manpower Research
and Analysis, Employment
Security Commission
P.O. Box 995
Columbia, SC 29202

South Dakota
Chief, Research and Statistics
Employment Security
Department
Department of Labor
700 Governors Dr.
Pierre, SD 57501

Tennessee
Chief, Research and Statistics
Department of Employment
Security
12th Floor, Volunteer Plaza
Bldg.
Nashville, TN 37245-0001

Texas
Chief, Economic Research
and Analysis
Employment Commission
101 E. 15th St.
Austin, TX 78778

Utah
Director, Research and
Analysis
Department of Employment
Security
P.O. Box 11249
Salt Lake City, UT 84147

Vermont
Chief, Research and Statistics
Department of Employment
Security
P.O. Box 488, Green Mt. Dr.
Montpelier, VT 05601-0488

Virginia
Commissioner
Virginia Employment
Commission
703 E. Main St.
Richmond, VA 23219

Washington
Chief, Research and Statistics
Employment Security
Department
212 Maple Park
Olympia, WA 98504

West Virginia
Chief, Labor and Economic
Research
Bureau of Employment
Programs
112 California Ave.
Charleston, WV 25305

Wisconsin
Director, Research and
Statistics
Department of Industry,
Labor and Human Relations
P.O. Box 7946
Madison, WI 53707

Wyoming
Chief, Research and Analysis
Department of Employment
Herschler Bldg., 2nd Floor E.
Cheyenne, WY 82002

Puerto Rico
Chief, Research and Statistics
Bureau of Employment
Security
427 Barbosa Ave.
Hato Rey, PR 00917

APPENDIX III
Government Employment

Many outdoor jobs can be found with various branches of the federal government. Some of these branches or departments are listed in this book, especially when they are primary employers for certain careers. If you wish to work for the federal government, it is helpful to first gain some understanding of the federal employment system.

The great majority of jobs with the federal government are regulated by the U.S. Office of Personnel Management (OPM). These are governed by civil service requirements, which include selection and advancement on the basis of merit; recruitment from all segments of society; and fair treatment without regard to differences of politics, race, color, national origin, religion, sex, marital status, age, or handicap. Constitutional rights and individual privacy are guaranteed, as are equal pay for work of equal value and high standards of integrity and conduct.

The federal government has several types of pay systems. One is the General Schedule (GS), which has consistent pay rates and covers professional, technical, and other white-collar positions. These positions are classified by their duties and the skills and responsibilities involved. This scale has eighteen pay grades; the higher numbers indicate greater responsibility and difficulty. The salary levels have fairly complex regulations, and attempts are made to grant increases in line with those given in private industry.

The other major pay system is the Federal Wage System, which covers trade, labor, and other blue-collar jobs. This pay system is not uniform throughout the country but is based on the rates of similar private-industry jobs in a specific geographic area. For this classification, the country is divided into 137 regions.

The OPM serves as the personnel agency for the government. Its duties include formulating policies and making certain that agencies are in compliance with personnel regulations.

The OPM also provides recruiting and examining functions for applicants for federal civil service employment. One of the first steps toward government employment is to file an application with the OPM and receive notice of the position level for which you qualify.

Information on the GS pay rates can be obtained from the nearest Federal Job Information Center (FJIC). Available federal jobs are listed in FJICs, as well as in various publications. There are about fifty FJICs throughout the country. You can locate the nearest one with the help of your telephone directory or local library.

Even after you are registered with the OPM, you may still need to take some initiative to get a job. You can learn about jobs from FJICs, but they are extremely busy and you may spend a lot of time waiting in line.

Another way to get a job with the government is to go directly to the local office of the agency that interests you. Each agency posts a listing of vacancies available, and it is where the hiring takes place. If you locate a job that interests you and you meet the requirements, you can submit an application directly to the agency. You can also request that the OPM consider your application for that position.

Competition is usually very keen for federal jobs, and if you are really interested in working for the government, it is worth taking the time to ensure that your application is processed for job vacancies that interest you. The standard government application form is the SF171. Careful and accurate completion of this form is a very important part of the process of being hired. Although you may be very qualified for a job, if the form does not present your qualifications well, you may not even be considered. Fill out the form very carefully with assistance from one of the books that offer help or from a career counselor.

This is only a brief introduction to the process of obtaining jobs with the federal government. It can be difficult and take a considerable amount of time. If working for the federal government is your goal, it will be worth your while to spend additional time researching the federal occupational classification system and learning how to fill out the SF171 to your best advantage. Check out some of the excellent books that are available on working for the government, including the ones listed in the Resources section of this appendix.

Resources

The following nongovernment periodicals list federal job vacancies and are available at libraries or by subscription.

Federal Career Opportunities, Federal Research Service, Inc., P.O. Box 1059-W, Vienna, VA 22180-1059. This biweekly publication lists about four thousand jobs.

Federal Jobs Digest, Federal Jobs Digest, Box 594, Millwood, NY 10546. This biweekly publication contains about fifteen thousand job listings.

Federal Times, Times Journal Company, Springfield, VA 22159-0190. This weekly publication has a small number of job listings but good articles relating to government jobs.

The following books explain the federal job hiring process and give some assistance with filling out the SF171.

Kraus, Krandall. *How to Get a Federal Job: A Guide to Finding and Applying for a Job with the U.S. Government Anywhere in the U.S.* New York: Facts on File Publications, 1986.

Waelde, David E. *How to Get a Federal Job.* Washington, DC: Fedhelp-Publications, 1987.

Index